Chuang Tzu
c. fourth century BC

Chuang Tzu
The Tao of Nature

TRANSLATED BY MARTIN PALMER WITH
ELIZABETH BREUILLY AND JAY RAMSAY

SELECTED BY MARTIN PALMER

PENGUIN BOOKS — GREAT IDEAS

PENGUIN BOOKS

Published by the Penguin Group
Penguin Books Ltd, 80 Strand, London WC2R ORL, England
Penguin Group (USA) Inc., 375 Hudson Street, New York, New York 10014, USA
Penguin Group (Canada), 90 Eglinton Avenue East, Suite 700, Toronto, Ontario,
Canada M4P 2Y3 (a division of Pearson Penguin Canada Inc.)
Penguin Ireland, 25 St Stephen's Green, Dublin 2, Ireland (a division of Penguin Books Ltd)
Penguin Group (Australia), 250 Camberwell Road, Camberwell, Victoria 3124, Australia
(a division of Pearson Australia Group Pty Ltd)
Penguin Books India Pvt Ltd, 11 Community Centre, Panchsheel Park,
New Delhi – 110 017, India
Penguin Group (NZ), 67 Apollo Drive, Rosedale, North Shore 0632, New Zealand
(a division of Pearson New Zealand Ltd)
Penguin Books (South Africa) (Pty) Ltd, 24 Sturdee Avenue, Rosebank, Johannesburg 2196,
South Africa

Penguin Books Ltd, Registered Offices: 80 Strand, London WC2R ORL, England

www.penguin.com

These extracts taken from *The Book of Chuang Tzu* first published by Arkana 1996
This selection published in Penguin Books 2010
1

Copyright © ICOREC, 1996, 2010
All rights reserved

Set in 11/13 pt Dante MT Std
Typeset by TexTech International
Printed in England by Clays Ltd, St Ives plc

ISBN: 978-0-141-19274-1

www.greenpenguin.co.uk

Mixed Sources
Product group from well-managed
forests and other controlled sources
www.fsc.org Cert no. SA-COC-1592
© 1996 Forest Stewardship Council

Penguin Books is committed to a sustainable future
for our business, our readers and our planet.
The book in your hands is made from paper
certified by the Forest Stewardship Council.

Contents

PART I

Working Everything Out Evenly

Now, I have something to say. Do I know whether this is in the same sort of category as what is said by others? I don't know. At one level, what I say is not the same. At another level, it most definitely is, and there is no difference between what I say and what others say. Whatever the case, let me try and tell you what I mean.

There is the beginning; there is not as yet any beginning of the beginning; there is not as yet beginning not to be a beginning of the beginning. There is what is, and there is what is not, and it is not easy to say whether what is not, is not; or whether what is, is.

I have just made a statement, yet I do not know whether what I said has been real in what I said or not really said.

Under Heaven there is nothing greater than the tip of a hair, but Mount Tai is smaller; there is no one older than a dead child, yet Peng Tsu died young.

Heaven and Earth and I were born at the same time, and all life and I are one.

As all life is one, what need is there for words? Yet I have just said all life is one, so I have already spoken, haven't I? One plus one equals two, two plus one equals three. To go on from here would take us beyond the understanding of even a skilled accountant, let alone the ordinary people. If going from 'no-thing' to 'some-thing' we get to three, just think how much further we would have to go if we went from 'some-thing' to something!

Don't even start, let's just stay put.

The great Tao has no beginning, and words have changed their meaning from the beginning, but because of the idea of a 'this is' there came to be limitations. I want to say something about these limitations. There is right and left, relationships and their consequences, divisions and disagreements, emulations and contentions. These are known as the eight Virtues.

The sage will not speak of what is beyond the boundaries of the universe – though he will not deny it either. What is within the universe, he says something about but does not pronounce upon. Concerning the record of the past actions of the kings in the *Spring and Autumn Annals*, the sage discusses but does not judge. When something is divided, something is not divided; when there is disagreement there are things not disagreed about.

You ask, what does this mean? The sage encompasses everything, while ordinary people just argue about things. This is why I say that disagreement means you do not understand at all.

> The great Way is not named,
> the great disagreement is unspoken,
> great benevolence is not benevolent,
> great modesty is not humble,
> great courage is not violent.
> The Tao that is clear is not the Tao,
> speech which enables argument is not worthy,

benevolence which is ever present does not
    achieve its goal,
modesty if flouted, fails,
courage that is violent is pointless.

[. . .]

Yeh Chueh said to Wang Ni, 'Do you know, Master, what everything agrees upon?'

'How can I possibly know?' said Wang Ni.

'Do you know, Master, what you do not know?'

'How can I know?' he replied.

'Then does nothing know anything?'

'How could I know that?' said Wang Ni. 'Nevertheless, I want to try and say something. How can I know that what I say I know is not actually what I don't know? Likewise, how can I know that what I think I don't know is not really what I do know? I want to put some questions to you:

'If someone sleeps in a damp place, he will ache all over and he will be half paralysed, but is it the same for an eel? If someone climbs a tree, he will be frightened and shaking, but is it so for a monkey? Out of these three, which is wisest about where to live?

'Humans eat meat, deer consume grass, centipedes devour snakes and owls and crows enjoy mice. Of these four, which has the best taste?

'Monkeys mate with each other, deer go with deer. People said that Mao Chiang and Li Chi were the most beautiful women in the world, but fish seeing them dived away, birds took off into the air and deer ran off. Of these four, who really knows true beauty? As I see it, benevolence and righteousness, also the ways of right and wrong, are completely interwoven. I do not think I can know the difference between them!'

Yeh Chueh said: 'Master, if you do not know the difference between that which is good and that which is harmful, does this mean the perfect man is also without such knowledge?'

'The perfect man is pure spirit,' replied Wang Ni. 'He does not feel the heat of the burning deserts nor the cold of the vast waters. He is not frightened by the lightning which can split open mountains, or by the storms that can whip up the seas. Such a person rides the clouds and mounts upon the sun and moon, and wanders across and beyond the four seas. Neither death nor life concern him, nor is he interested in what is good or bad!'

Chu Chiao Tzu asked Chang Wu Tzu,

> 'I have heard from the Master
> that the sage does not labour at anything,
> does not look for advantage,
> does not act benevolently,
> does not harm,
> does not pursue the Tao;
> He speaks without speaking,
> and does not speak when he speaks,
> and looks beyond the confines of this
> dusty world.

'The Master sees all this as an endless stream of words,

but to me they are like the words of the mysterious Tao. Master, what do you think?'

Chang Wu Tzu said, 'Such a saying as this would have confused even the Yellow Emperor, so how could Confucius be able to understand them! However, you are getting ahead of yourself, counting your chickens before your eggs are hatched and looking at the bowl, imagining the roasted fowl. I will try to speak to you in a random way, so you listen to me likewise. How can the wise one sit beside the sun and moon and embrace the universe? Because he brings all things together in harmony, he rejects difference and confusion and ignores status and power. While ordinary people rush busily around, the sage seems stupid and ignorant, but to him all life is one and united. All life is simply what it is and all appear to him to be doing what they rightly should.

'How do I know that the love of life is not a delusion? Or that the fear of death is not like a young person running away from home and unable to find his way back? The Lady Li Chi was the daughter of a border warden, Ai. When the state of Chin captured her, she wept until she had drenched her robes; then she came to the King's palace, shared the King's bed, ate his food, and repented of her tears. How do I know whether the dead now repent for their former clinging to life?

'Come the morning, those who dream of the drunken feast may weep and moan; when the morning comes, those who dream of weeping and moaning go hunting in the fields. When they dream, they don't know it is a dream. Indeed, in their dreams they may think they are interpreting dreams, only when they awake do they know it was a dream. Eventually there comes the day of reckoning and awakening, and then we shall know that it was all a great dream. Only fools think that they are now awake and that they really know what is going on, playing the prince and then playing the servant. What fools! The Master and you are both living in a dream. When I say a dream, I am also dreaming. This very saying is a deception. If after ten thousand years we could once meet a truly great sage, one who understands, it would seem as if it had only been a morning.

'Imagine that you and I have a disagreement, and you get the better of me, rather than me getting the better of you, does this mean that you are automatically right and I am automatically wrong? Suppose I get the better of you, does it follow that I am automatically right and you are therefore wrong? Is it really that one of us is right and the other wrong? Or are we both right and both wrong? Neither you nor I can really know and other people are even more in the dark. So who can we ask to give us the right answer? Should you ask someone who thinks you are right? But how then can that person give a fair answer? Should we ask someone who thinks I am right? But then if he agrees with me, how can he make a fair judgement? Then again, should we ask someone who agrees with both of us? But again, if he agrees with both of us, how can he make a true judgement? Should we ask someone who disagrees with both of us? But here again, if he disagrees with both of us, how can he make an honest judgement? It is clear that neither you, I nor anyone else can make decisions like this amongst ourselves. So should we wait for someone else to turn up?

'To wait for one voice to bring it all together is as pointless as waiting for no one. Bring all things together under the Equality of Heaven, allow their process of change to go on unimpeded, and learn to grow old. What do I mean by bringing everything together under the Equality of Heaven? With regard to what is right and wrong, I say not being is being and being is not being. But let us not get caught up in discussing this. Forget about life, forget about worrying about right and wrong. Plunge into the unknown and the endless and find your place there!'

The Outline said to the Shadow, 'First you are on the move, then you are standing still; you sit down and then you stand up. Why can't you make up your mind?'

Shadow replied, 'Do I have to look to something else to be what I am? Does this something else itself not have to rely upon yet another something? Do I have to depend upon the scales of a snake or the wings of a cicada? How can I tell how things are? How can I tell how things are not?'

Once upon a time, I, Chuang Tzu, dreamt that I was a butterfly, flitting around and enjoying myself. I had no idea I was Chuang Tzu. Then suddenly I woke up and was Chuang Tzu again. But I could not tell, had I been Chuang Tzu dreaming I was a butterfly, or a butterfly dreaming I was now Chuang Tzu? However, there must be some sort of difference between Chuang Tzu and a butterfly! We call this the transformation of things.

PART 2

Perfect Accord

Cook Ting was butchering an ox for Lord Wen Hui. Every movement of his hand, every shrug of his shoulder, every step of his feet, every thrust of his knee, every sound of the sundering flesh and the swoosh of the descending knife, were all in perfect accord, like the Mulberry Grove Dance or the rhythm of the Ching-shou.

'Ah, how excellent!' said Lord Wen Hui. 'How has your skill become so superb?'

Cook Ting put down his knife and said, 'What your servant loves best is the Tao, which is better than any art. When I started to cut up oxen, what I saw was just a complex ox. After three years, I had learnt not to see the ox as whole. Now I practise with my mind, not with my eyes. I ignore my sense and follow my spirit. I see the natural lines and my knife slides through the great hollows, follows the great cavities, using that which is already there to my advantage. Thus, I miss the great sinews and even more so, the great bones. A good cook changes his knife annually, because he slices. An ordinary cook has to change his knife every month, because he hacks. Now this knife of mine I have been using for nineteen years, and it has cut thousands of oxen. However, its blade is as sharp as if it had just been sharpened. Between the joints there are spaces, and the blade of a knife has no real thickness. If you put what has no thickness into spaces such as these, there is plenty of room, certainly enough for the knife to work through. However, when I come to a difficult part and can see that it will be difficult, I take care and pay due regard. I look carefully and I move with caution. Then, very gently, I move the knife until there is a parting and the flesh falls apart like a lump of earth falling to the ground. I stand with the knife in my hand looking around and then, with an air of satisfaction, I wipe the knife and put it away.'

'Splendid!' said Lord Wen Hui. 'I have heard what cook Ting has to say and from his words I have learned how to live life fully.'

When Kung Wen Hsien saw the Commander of the Right he was surprised and said, 'Who is this man? Why has he only got one foot? Is this from Heaven or from man?'

'From Heaven, not from man,' said the Commander. 'My life came from Heaven, which also gave me just one foot. The human appearance is a gift, which is why I know that this is from Heaven, not from man. The marsh pheasant manages one peck every ten paces, and one drink every hundred steps, but it does not wish to be kept in a cage. Even if you treated it like a king, its spirit would not be happy.'

When Lao Tzu died, Chin Shih came to mourn for him. He uttered three shouts and then left.

A follower of the Master said, 'Wasn't the Master a friend of yours?'

'Certainly,' he replied.

'Then do you really think this way of mourning is best?'

'Certainly. To begin with I thought these were real men, but now I am not so sure. When I came in to mourn, there were old folk weeping as though they had lost a child; there were young people wailing as if for the loss of a mother. Such a gathering of everyone, all talking away though he didn't ask them to talk and weeping even though he didn't ask for tears! This is to turn from Heaven and to indulge in emotions, ignoring what is given. The ancient ones called this the result of violating the principles of Heaven. When the Master came, it was because he was due to be born. When he died, it was entirely natural. If you are prepared to accept this and flow with it, then sorrow and joy cannot touch you. The ancient ones considered this the work of the gods who free us from bondage.

'We can point to the wood that has been burned, but when the fire has passed on, we cannot know where it has gone.'

[. . .]

Yen Ho was about to start as tutor to the eldest son of Duke Ling of the state of Wei, so he went to visit Chu Po Yu and said, 'Here is a man whom Heaven has given a nature devoid of all virtue. If I simply allow him to go on in this way, the state is at risk; if I try to bring him back to a principled life, then my life is at risk. He can just about recognize the excesses of others, but not his own excesses. In a case like this, what can I do?'

'This is a good question!' said Chu Po Yu. 'Be on guard, be careful, make sure you yourself are right. Let your appearance be in agreement, let your heart be content and harmonious. However, both these strategies have their dangers. Do not let your outward stance affect your inner self, nor allow your inner self to be drawn out. If you allow yourself to be sucked into his way of things, you will be thrown down, ruined, demolished, and will fall. If your inner harmony becomes drawn out, then you will have fame and a name, you will be called an evil creature. If he acts like a child, then be a child with him; if he permits no restraints, do the same. If he goes beyond the pale, follow him! Understand him, and then guide him back subtly.

'Don't you know the story of the praying mantis? In its anger it waved its arms in front of a speeding carriage, having no understanding that it could not stop it, but having full confidence in its own powers! Be on guard, be careful! If you are over-confident in this way, you will be in the same danger.

'Don't you know what a tiger trainer does? He does not give them living animals for food, in case it over-excites them and breeds a love of killing. He does not even give them whole carcasses, for fear of exciting the rage of tearing the animals apart. He observes their appetite and appreciates their ferocity. Tigers are a different creature from humans, but you can train them to obey their trainer if you understand how to adapt to them. People who go against the nature of the tiger don't last long.

'People who love horses collect their manure and urine in fine baskets and bottles. However, if a mosquito or gadfly lands on the horse, and the groom suddenly swipes it away, the horse breaks its bit, damages its harness and hurts its chest. The groom, out of affection, tried to do what was good, but the end result is the reverse of that. Thus should we exercise caution!'

Carpenter Shih was on his way to Chi, when he came to the place called Chu Yuan, where he saw an oak tree which was venerated as the home of the spirits of the land. The tree was so vast that a thousand oxen could hide behind it. It was a hundred spans round and it soared above the hill to eighty feet before it even began to put out branches. There were ten such branches, from any one of which an entire boat could be carved. Masses of people came to see it, giving the place a carnival atmosphere, but carpenter Shih didn't even look round, just went on his way. His assistant looked at it with great intensity, and then chased after his master and said, 'Since I first took up my axe and followed you, I have never seen wood such as this. Sir, why did you not even glance at it nor stop, but just kept going?'

He said, 'Silence, not another word! The tree is useless. Make a boat from it and it would sink; make a coffin and it would rot quickly; make some furniture and it would fall to pieces; make a door and it would be covered in seeping sap; make a pillar and it would be worm-eaten. This wood is useless and good for nothing. This is why it has lived so long.'

When Master Shih was returning, the tree appeared to him in a dream, saying, 'What exactly are you comparing me with? With ornamental fruit trees? Trees such as the hawthorn, pear trees, orange trees, citrus trees, gourds and other such fruit trees? Their fruits are knocked down when they are ripe and the trees suffer. The big branches are damaged and the small ones are broken off. Because they are useful, they suffer, and they are unable to live out the years Heaven has given them. They have only their usefulness to blame for this destruction wrought by the people. It is the same with all things. I have spent a long time studying to be useless, though on a couple of occasions I was nearly destroyed. However, now I have perfected the art of uselessness, and this is very useful, to me! If I had been of use, could I have grown so vast? Furthermore, you and I are both things. How can one thing make such statements about another? How can you, a useless man about to die, know anything about a useless tree?'

When carpenter Shih awoke, he told his apprentice what he had dreamt. The apprentice said, 'If it wants to be useless, why is it used as the shrine for the spirits of the land?'

'Hush! Don't say another word!' said Shih. 'The tree happens to be here so it is an altar. By this it protects itself from harm from those who do not realize it is useless, for were it not an altar, it would run the risk of being chopped down. Furthermore, this tree is no ordinary one, so to speak of it in normal terms is to miss the point.'

Nan Po Tzu Chi, wandering amongst the mountains of Shang, came upon a great and unusual tree, under which could shelter a thousand chariots, and they would all be covered. Tzu Chi said, 'What kind of a tree is this? It is surely a most wondrous piece of timber!' However, when he looked up, he could see that the smaller branches were so twisted and gnarled that they could not be made into rafters and beams; and looking down at the trunk he saw it was warped and distorted and would not make good coffins. He licked one of its leaves and his mouth felt scraped and sore. He sniffed it and it nearly drove him mad, as if he had been drunk for three days.

'This tree is certainly good for nothing,' said Tzu Chi. 'This is why it has grown so large. Ah-ha! This is the sort of uselessness that sages live by.

'In the state of Sung there is the district of Ching Shih, which is excellent for growing catalpas, cypresses and mulberry trees. However, those which are more than a handspan or so around are cut down by people who want to make posts for their monkeys; those which are three or four spans around are cut down to make beams for great houses; those of seven to eight spans are cut down by lords and the wealthy who want single planks to form the side of their coffins. As a result, the trees do not live out the years Heaven has allotted them, but instead are cut down by the axe in the prime of their life. This is all the result of being useful! At the sacrifice, oxen marked by the white forehead, pigs that have turned-up noses and men suffering from piles are useless as offerings to the River Ho. Shamans know this and as a result they consider such creatures as being inauspicious. However, the sage, for exactly this same reason, values them highly.

'Crippled Shu, now, is a man with his chin lost in his navel, his shoulders higher than the top of his head and his topknot pointing to Heaven, his five vital organs all crushed into the top of his body and his two thighs pressing into his ribs. By sharpening needles and washing clothes he earns enough to eat. By winnowing rice and cleaning it he was able to feed ten people. When the officials called up the militia, he walked about freely, with no need to hide; when they are trying to raise a large work gang, because of his deformities, no one bothers him. Yet when the officials were handing out grain to the infirm, he received three great portions and ten bundles of firewood. If a man like this, deformed in body, can make a living and live out the years Heaven sends him, how much more should a man who is only deformed in terms of his Virtue!'

[. . .]

In the state of Lu there was a mutilated man called Shu Shan the Toeless. He came upon his stumps to see Confucius. Confucius said, 'You were not careful and therefore suffered this fate. It is too late to come and see me now.'

'Because of my lack of knowledge and through lack of care for my body, I lost my feet,' said Toeless. 'Now I have come to you because I still have that which is of greater value than my foot and I wish to save it. There is nothing that great Heaven does not cover, nor anything that the Earth does not sustain. I had hoped you, Sir, would be as Heaven and Earth to me, and I did not expect you to receive me like this!'

'I am being stupid!' said Confucius. 'Good Sir, please do not go away and I will try to share with you what I have learnt!'

However, Toeless left and Confucius said, 'Be watchful, my followers! Great Toeless has lost his feet but still he wants to learn in order to recompense for his evil deeds. How much more so should you who are able-bodied want to learn!'

Toeless told his story to Lao Tzu, saying, 'Confucius has definitely not become a perfect man yet, has he? So why does he try to study with you? He seems to be caught up with the search for honour and reputation, without appearing to understand that the perfect man sees these as chains and irons.'

Lao Tzu said, 'Why not help him to see that death and birth are one thing and that right and wrong are one thing, and so free him from the chains and irons?'

'Given that Heaven punishes him, how can he be set free?' asked Toeless.

Duke Ai of Lu said to Confucius, 'In Wei there was a man with a terrible appearance called Ai Tai To. But those around him thought the world of him and when women saw him they ran to their mothers and fathers saying, "I would rather be the concubine of this gentleman than anyone else's wife." This has happened more than ten times. He was never heard to take the lead in anything, but was always in accord with others. He was not powerful and thus able to save people from death, nor was he wealthy and able to feed people. Furthermore, he was so hideous he could scare the whole world. He never took the lead, just agreed with whatever was suggested, and he knew little about the world beyond his own four walls. But people came flocking to him. It is clear he is different from ordinary people, so I asked him to come and see me. He certainly was ugly enough to frighten the whole world. Yet he had only been with me for less than a month when I began to appreciate him.

Within a year I had full trust in him. In my country there was no prime minister, so I offered him the post. His response to my request was to look most sorrowful and diffident as if he was going to turn it down. I was ashamed of myself but in the end simply handed over the country to him. Very soon after, he upped and left. I was distressed and felt this a great loss, for I had no one with whom to share the cares of the state. Now, what sort of man is this?'

Confucius said, 'I was once in the state of Chu on a commission, and I saw some piglets trying to suckle from their dead mother. After a while they started up and left her. She did not seem to notice them and so they no longer felt any affinity with her. What they loved about their mother was not her body but what gave life to the body. When a man is killed in battle, at his burial his battle honours are of little use to him. A man without feet has little love for shoes. In both cases they lack that which makes these of any significance. Indeed, the consorts of the Son of Heaven do not cut their own nails or pierce their ears; a newly wed gentleman stays outside the court and is freed from onerous duties. With so much attention being paid to caring for the body, imagine what care should be given to preserving Virtue! Now Ai Tai To speaks not a word, yet he is believed. He does nothing and is loved. People offer him their kingdoms, and their only fear is that he will refuse. He must indeed be a man of perfect character, whose Virtue is without shape!'

'What do you mean by "perfect character"?' asked Duke Ai.

Confucius replied, 'Death, birth, existence and trouble, auspicious and inauspicious signs, wealth, poverty, value and worthlessness, glory and blame, hunger and thirst, cold and hot – all these are the way the world goes and the result of destiny. Day and night follow each other, but there is no way of knowing where they come from. Don't allow this to disrupt your innate balance, don't allow this to perturb your mind. If you can balance and enjoy them, have mastery over them and revel in this, if you can do this day in and day out without a break and bring all things together, then this brings forth a heart prepared for changes and this is perfect character.'

'But what do you mean when you say his Virtue is without shape?'

'Perfect balance is found in still waters. Such water should be an example to us all. Inner harmony is protected and nothing external affects it. Virtue is the result of true balance. Virtue has no shape or form yet nothing can be without it,' said Confucius.

PART 3

So What is a True Man?

The one who understands Heaven and understands the ways of humanity has perfection. Understanding Heaven, he grows with Heaven. Understanding humanity, he takes the understanding of what he understands to help him understand what he doesn't understand, and so fulfils the years Heaven decrees without being cut off in his prime. This is known as perfection.

However, it is true that there are problems. Real understanding has to have something to which it is applied and this something is itself uncertain. So how can I know that what I term Heaven is not human? Or that what I call human is not Heaven?

Only the true man has understanding. So what is a true man? The true man of old did not fight against poverty, nor did he look for fulfilment through riches – for he had no grand plans. Therefore, he never regretted any failure, nor exulted in success. He could scale the heights without fear, plumb the depths without difficulties and go through fire without pain. This is the kind of person whose understanding has lifted him up towards the Tao.

The true man of old slept without dreaming and awoke without anxiety. He ate without tasting, breathing deeply, incredibly deeply. The true man breathes from his feet up, while ordinary people just breathe from the throat. The words of broken people come forth like vomit. Wallowing in lust and desire, they are but shallow in the ways of Heaven.

The true man of old did not hold on to life, nor did he fear death. He arrived without expectation and left without resistance. He went calmly, he came calmly and that was that. He did not set out to forget his origin, nor was he interested in what would become of him. He loved to receive anything but also forgot what he had received and gave it away. He did not give precedence to the heart but to the Tao, nor did he prefer the ways of humanity to those of Heaven. This is what is known as a true man.

> Being like this, his heart forgets,
> his appearance is calm,
> his forehead is plain;
> He is as chilly as autumn and as warming as spring.
> His joy and anger arise like the four seasons.
> He acts properly towards all things
> and none know where this will lead.
> So if the sage summons the army and conquers states,
> he does not lose the affections of the people.
> His magnanimous nature enriches ten
>   thousand generations,
> yet he has no affection for the people.
> One who seeks to share his happiness with others
>   is not a sage.
> One who displays his feelings is not benevolent.
> One who waits for Heaven is not a wise man.
> The noble who cannot harmonize the good and the
>   destructive is not a scholar.

So What is a True Man?

One who seeks for fame and thereby loses his
    real self is no gentleman.
One who loses his true self and his path is unable
    to command others.
[. . .]
The true man of old appeared aloof but was in no
    danger of falling.
He appears deficient, yet takes nothing.
He does what he wills but is not judgemental.
His emptiness was clear, but there was no showing off.
Cheerfully smiling, he seemed to be content.
He responded immediately as if there was no choice.
If upset, he showed it.
If content, he was at ease with Virtue.
When calm, he appeared to be one with the world.
When superior, the world had no control over him.
His inner nature seemed unknowable.
Never being really aware, he forgot what to say.
He saw the law as the external form of government.
The rituals he saw as the wings,
knowledge as being the same as what is appropriate
    at the time.
Virtue he saw as what is proper.
Viewing law as the external form of government,
he was flexible in imposing the death sentence.
Viewing the rituals as the wings,
he got on well with society.
Viewing knowledge as being that which
    is appropriate,
he followed the natural course of events.
Viewing virtue as that which is proper,

he walked along with others who were capable
    of leading.
So he acted spontaneously,
but others thought it was at great cost.
Thus all that he sought was one.
What he disowned was also but one.
What is one is one, and what is not one is also one.
In the one, he was with Heaven.
In the not-one, he was one with humanity.
When heaven and humanity are not in dispute,
then we can say this is really the true man.

Death and birth are fixed. They are as certain as the dawn
that comes after the night, established by the decree of
Heaven. This is beyond the control of humanity, this is just
how things are. Some view Heaven as their father and continue to love it. How much more should they show devotion
for that which is even greater! Some people consider their
lord as being better than themselves and would willingly die
for him. How much more should they do the same for one
who is more true than their lord!

When the springs dry out, the fish are found stranded
on the earth. They keep each other damp with their own
moisture, and wet each other with their slime. But it
would be better if they could just forget about each other
in rivers and lakes. People sing the praises of Yao and condemn Chieh, but it would be better if they could forget
both of them and just follow the Tao. The cosmos gives
me the burden of a physical form, makes life a struggle,
gives me rest in old age and peace in death. What makes
life good, therefore, also makes death good.

A boat can be hidden in a gorge, and a fishing net in a pool, and you may think they are therefore safe. However, in the middle of the night a strong man comes and carries them off. Small-minded people just cannot see that hiding smaller things in larger things does not mean they will not be stolen. If you take everything under Heaven and try to store it under Heaven, there is no space left for it to be lost in! This is the real truth about things. To have a human form is a joyful thing. But in the universe of possible forms, there are others just as good. Isn't it a blessing to have these uncountable possibilities! The sage goes where nothing escapes him, and rests contented there with them. He takes pleasure in an early death, in old age, in the origin and in the end and sees them all as equally good – he should be an example to others. If this is so, then how much more should our example be that which holds together the whole of life and which is the origin of all that changes!

The great Tao has both reality and expression, but it does nothing and has no form.

> It can be passed on, but not received.
> It can be obtained, but not seen.
> It is rooted in its own self, existing before Heaven
>   and Earth were born, indeed for eternity.
> It gives divinity to the spirits and to the gods.
> It brought to life Heaven and Earth.
> It was before the primal air, yet it cannot be
>   called lofty;
> it was below all space and direction, yet it cannot
>   be called deep.

It comes before either Heaven or Earth, yet it
    cannot be called old.
It is far more ancient than antiquity, yet it is not old.

[. . .]

The Masters, Ssu, Yu, Li and Lai, said one to another, 'Anyone who can conceive of nothingness as his head, life as his back and death as his tail and who knows that death and birth, being and no-being, are one and the same – one like this shall be our friend.' The four men smiled and agreed in their hearts and therefore became friends.

Shortly after, Master Yu fell ill. Master Ssu went to visit him and Yu said, 'How great is the Maker of All! He has made me deformed. My back is like a hunchback's, and all my organs are on top while my chin is lost in my navel and my shoulders rise up above my head and my topknot points to Heaven!' His yin and yang were in disarray. However, his heart was calm and he was not worried. He limped to a well and looked in at his reflection and said, 'Goodness me! The Maker of All has made me completely deformed!'

'Do you dislike it?' asked Master Ssu.

'Not really, why should I? For example, perhaps my left arm will become a cockerel and then I shall be able to tell the time at night. Maybe, eventually, my right arm will become a crossbow and then I can hunt a bird and eat it. Possibly my bottom will become wheels and my soul will be a horse which I shall climb upon and go for a ride. After all, I wouldn't then need any other vehicle again! I obtained life because the time was right. I will lose life because it is time. Those who go quietly with the flow of nature are not worried by either joy or sorrow. People like these were considered in the past as having achieved freedom from bondage. Those who cannot free themselves are constrained by things. However, nothing can overcome Heaven – it has always been so. So why should I dislike this?'

Later Master Lai fell ill. Gasping and heaving, he lay close to death. His wife and children were mourning around him. Master Li came to see him and Master Lai said, 'Hush, get out! Do you want to disrupt the processes of change?'

Leaning against the doorway Li commented,

'How great is the Maker of All!
What will you be made into next?
Where will you be sent?
Will you come back as a rat's liver?
Or will it be as a pest's arm?'

Master Lai said,

'When a mother and father tell a child to
   go somewhere,
be that east, west, south or north, the child obeys.
Yin and yang are the mother and father of humanity.
They have brought me close to death
and if I disobey this would be just perversity.
My death is not their problem!
The cosmos gives me form, brings me to birth,
guides me into old age and settles me in death.

33

If I think my life good, then I must think my
    death good.
A good craftsman, casting metal,
would not be too pleased with metal that
    jumped up and said,
"I must be made into a sword like Mo Yeh."
Now, given that I have been bold enough
to take on human shape already, if I then said,
"I must be a human, I must be a human!",
the Maker of All would view me somewhat askance!
If Heaven and Earth are like a furnace and Nature
    is the craftsman,
then is it possible he could send me anywhere
    that was not appropriate?
Peacefully we die, calmly we awake.'

PART 4

Simply Fate!

Masters Yu and Sang were friends. It happened to rain for ten days, and Master Yu said, 'Master Sang may be in trouble!' So he packed some food to take to him. Arriving at Master Sang's door he heard strange noises and someone playing a lute, singing,

'Oh Father! Oh Mother! Oh Heaven! Oh humanity!'

It sounded as if the singer's voice was about to break and the singer was rushing to finish the verse. Master Yu entered and said, 'Master, why are you singing like this?'

He said, 'I was trying to work out what has reduced me to this. My father and mother wouldn't want me to be so poor, surely? Heaven treats all alike. Earth supports all alike. Heaven and Earth wouldn't wish me poor, would they? I seek to know who has done this, but I can't find an answer. When you come down to it, it must be simply fate.'

[. . .]

Tien Ken was travelling to the south of Yin Mountain. He reached the river Liao, where he met the Man without a Name and said to him, 'I wish to ask you about governing everything under Heaven.'

The Man without a Name said, 'Get lost, you stupid lout! What an unpleasant question! I am travelling with the Maker of All. If that is too tiring, I shall ride the bird of ease and emptiness and go beyond the compass of the world and wander in the land of nowhere and the region of nothing. So why are you disturbing me and unsettling my heart with questions about how to rule all below Heaven?'

Tien Ken asked the same question again. The Man without a Name replied.

> 'Let your heart journey in simplicity.
> Be one with that which is beyond definition.
> Let things be what they are.
> Have no personal views.
> This is how everything under Heaven is ruled.'

Yan Tzu Chu went to visit Lao Tzu and he said, 'Here is a man who is keen and vigilant, who has clarity of vision and wisdom and who studies the Tao without ceasing. Such a person as this is surely a king of great wisdom?'

'In comparison to the sage,' said Lao Tzu, 'someone like this is just a humble servant, tied to his work, exhausting himself and distressing his heart. The tiger and the leopard, it is said, are hunted because of the beauty of their hides. The monkey and the dog end up in chains because of their skills. Can these be compared to a king of great wisdom?'

Yang Tzu Chu was startled and said, 'May I be so bold as to ask about the rule of a king who is great in wisdom?'

Lao Tzu said,

'The rule of a king who is great in wisdom!
   His works affect all under Heaven, yet he seems
      to do nothing.
   His authority reaches all life, yet no one relies
      upon him.
   There is no fame or glory for him but everything
      fulfils itself.
   He stands upon mystery and wanders where
      there is nothing.'

In Chen there was a shaman of the spirits called Chi Hsien. He could foretell when people would die and be born; he knew about good fortune and failure as granted by Heaven; he knew about happiness and distress, life and its span, knowing the year, month, week and day, as if he were a god himself. As soon as the people of Cheng saw him coming, they would run away. Lieh Tzu went to see him and was fascinated by him. Coming back to Hu Tzu, he said, 'I used to believe, Master, that your Tao was perfection. Now I have found something even better.'

Hu Tzu said, 'What I have shown you is the outward text of my teaching, but not what is central. How can you think you have grasped my Tao? If you have hens but no cockerel, how can you have eggs? You flaunt your Tao before the world. This is why this man can read your fortune. Bring this shaman to me and let us meet.'

The next day Lieh Tzu brought the shaman to visit Hu Tzu. And as he left Hu Tzu's house with Lieh Tzu, the shaman said, 'Oh dear! Your Master is dying. There's virtually no life left – he has maybe a week at most. I saw a strange sight – it was like wet ashes!'

Lieh Tzu went in again, weeping so copiously that tears soaked his coat, and told Hu Tzu what had been said. Hu Tzu said, 'I made myself appear like the earth. I was as solid as the mountain, showing nothing to him. He probably perceived me to be a closed book, apparently without virtue. Bring him again if you can.'

The next day Lieh Tzu came again with the shaman to see Hu Tzu. As they went out, the shaman said to Lieh Tzu, 'How lucky for your Master that he has met me. He is getting better. Indeed he is truly alive. Life is flowing again.'

Lieh Tzu went back in and commented on this to Hu Tzu. Hu Tzu said, 'I made myself appear to him like Heaven, without fame or fortune on my mind. What I am wells up in me naturally. He saw in me the full and natural workings of life. Bring him again if you can.'

The next day they came again to see Hu Tzu. As they went out, the shaman said to Lieh Tzu, 'Your Master is never the same. I cannot grasp the fortune shown in his face. If he returns to some constancy then I will come and see him again.'

Lieh Tzu went back in and reported this to Hu Tzu. 'I showed him myself as the great Void where all is equal,' said Hu Tzu. 'He almost certainly saw in me the harmony of my innate forces. When water moves about, there is a whirlpool; where the waters are calm, there is a whirlpool; where the waters gather, there is a whirlpool. There are nine types of whirlpool and I have shown him just three. Bring him back again if you can.'

The next day they both came again to see him. However, before he had even sat down, the shaman panicked and ran off. Hu Tzu said, 'Follow him!'

Lieh Tzu ran after him. But he could not catch up with him. Coming back to Hu Tzu, he said, 'He has gone, I've lost him. I couldn't catch him.'

Hu Tzu said, 'I just appeared to him as hitherto unrevealed potential. I presented myself as not knowing who is who, nor what is what. I came flowing and changing as I willed. That's why he bolted.'

As a result of this, Lieh Tzu realized that he had so far learnt nothing real, so he returned home. For three years he did not go out. He cooked for his wife and tended the pigs as if they were humans. He showed no interest in his studies. He cast aside his desires and sought the truth. In his body he became like the ground itself. In the midst of everything he remained enclosed with the One and that is how he remained until the end.

> Do not hanker for fame.
> Do not make plans.
> Do not try to do things.
> Do not try to master knowledge.
> Hold what is but do not hold it to be anything.
> Work with all that comes from Heaven, but do
>   not seek to hold it.
> Just be empty.
>
> The perfect man's heart is like a mirror.
> It does not search after things.
> It does not look for things.

It does not seek knowledge, just responds.
As a result he can handle everything and is not
   harmed by anything.
[. . .]
One on the true path does not lose his innate
   given nature.
To such a man that which is united presents
   no problem;
That which is divided is all right;
What is long is not too long;
That which is short is not too short.
The duck's legs for example are short, but
   trying to lengthen them would cause pain.
The legs of a crane are long, but trying to
   shorten them would produce grief.
What nature makes long we should not cut,
nor should we try to stretch what nature
   makes short.
That would not solve anything.

Perhaps then, benevolence and righteousness are not
an inherent part of human nature? For look how much
anxiety is suffered by those who wish to be kind.

PART 5

Hui Tzu

Hui Tzu spoke to Chuang Tzu, saying, 'The King of Wei gave me the seeds of an enormous gourd, which I planted and it produced a fruit big enough to hold five bushels of anything, so I used it to hold water, but it was then too heavy to pick up. I cut it into two to make scoops, but they were too awkward to use. It was not that they weren't big, I just found I could not make use of them, so I destroyed them.'

Chuang Tzu said, 'Dear Sir, surely the problem is that you don't know how to use big things. There is a man in Sung who could make a cream which prevented the hands from getting chapped, and generation after generation of his family have made a living by bleaching silk. A pilgrim heard this and offered to buy the secret for a hundred pieces of gold. All the family came together to respond and said, "For generation after generation we have bleached silk, yet we have never made more than a few pieces of gold; now in just one morning we can earn a hundred pieces of gold! Let's do it." So the pilgrim got the secret and went to see the King of Wu. He was struggling with the state of Yueh. The King of Wu gave the pilgrim command of the army and in the depths of winter they fought the men of Yueh on the water, inflicting a crushing blow on the forces of Yueh, and the traveller was rewarded by the gift of a vast estate from the conquered territory. The cream had stopped the hands chapping in both cases: one gained an estate, but the others had never got further than bleaching silk, because they used this secret in such different ways. Now, Sir, you have a gourd big enough to hold five bushels, so why didn't you use it to make big bottles which could help you float down the rivers and lakes, instead of dismissing it as being useless? Because, dear Sir, your head is full of straw!'

Hui Tzu spoke to Chuang Tzu, saying, 'I have a big tree, which people call useless. Its trunk is so knotted, no carpenter could work on it, while its branches are too twisted to use a square or compass upon. So, although it is close to the road, no carpenter would look at it. Now, Sir, your words are like this, too big and no use, therefore everyone ignores them.'

Chuang Tzu said, 'Sir, have you never seen a wild cat or weasel? It lies there, crouching and waiting; east and west it leaps out, not afraid of going high or low; until it is caught in a trap and dies in a net. Yet again, there is the yak, vast like a cloud in heaven. It is big, but cannot use this fact to catch rats. Now you, Sir, have a large tree, and you don't know how to use it, so why not plant it in the middle of nowhere, where you can go to wander or fall asleep under its shade? No axe under Heaven will attack it, nor shorten its days, for something which is useless will never be disturbed.'

[. . .]

Hui Tzu asked Chuang Tzu, 'Is it possible for someone to be without emotion?'

'Certainly,' said Chuang Tzu.

'A man without emotion – can you really call him a man?' asked Hui Tzu.

Chuang Tzu replied, 'The Way gives him a face and Heaven provides a shape, so how can it follow he is not called a man?'

'But if he is already called a man, how can it follow that he has no emotion?'

'That's not what I mean by emotions,' said Chuang Tzu. 'When I say a man has no emotions, what I mean by this is someone who does not allow either the good or the bad to have any effect upon him. He lets all things be and allows life to continue in its own way.'

Hui Tzu said, 'If he doesn't interfere with life, then how does he take care of himself?'

'The Way gives him a face and Heaven provides a shape. He does not allow either the good or the bad to have any effect on him. But you now, you wear your soul on your sleeve, exhausting your energy, propping yourself up on a tree, mumbling, or bent over your desk, asleep. Heaven gives you a form and you wear it out by pointless argument!'

[. . .]

Hui Tzu was made Minister of State in Liang and Chuang Tzu went to see him. Someone told Hui Tzu, 'Chuang Tzu is coming, because he wants to oust you from your office.' This alarmed Hui Tzu and he scoured the kingdom for three days and nights trying to find this stranger.

Chuang Tzu went to see him and said, 'In the south there is a bird known as the Young Phoenix, do you know about this, Sir? This bird, it arises in the Southern Ocean and flies to the Northern Ocean and it never rests on anything except the begonia tree, never eats except the fruit of the melia azederach and never drinks except from springs of sweet water. There was once an owl who had clutched in his talons a rotting rat corpse. As the Young Phoenix flew overhead the owl looked up and said, "Shoo!" Now you, Sir, you have the state of Liang and you feel you have to shoo me away?'

Chuang Tzu and Hui Tzu were walking beside the weir on the River Hao, when Chuang Tzu said, 'Do you see how the fish are coming to the surface and swimming around as they please? That's what fish really enjoy.'

'You're not a fish,' replied Hui Tzu, 'so how can you say you know what fish enjoy?'

Chuang Tzu said: 'You are not me, so how can you know I don't know what fish enjoy?'

Hui Tzu said: 'I am not you, so I definitely don't know what it is you know. However, you are most definitely not a fish and that proves that you don't know what fish really enjoy.'

Chuang Tzu said: 'Ah, but let's return to the original question you raised, if you don't mind. You asked me how I could know what it is that fish really enjoy. Therefore, you already knew I knew it when you asked the question. And I know it by being here on the edge of the River Hao.'

[. . .]

Chuang Tzu's wife died and Hui Tzu came to console him, but Chuang Tzu was sitting, legs akimbo, bashing a battered tub and singing.

Hui Tzu said, 'You lived as man and wife, she reared your children. At her death surely the least you should be doing is to be on the verge of weeping, rather than banging the tub and singing: this is not right!'

Chuang Tzu said, 'Certainly not. When she first died, I certainly mourned just like everyone else! However, I then thought back to her birth and to the very roots of her being, before she was born. Indeed, not just before she was born but before the time when her body was created. Not just before her body was created but before the very origin of her life's breath. Out of all this, through the wonderful mystery of change she was given her life's breath. Her life's breath wrought a transformation and she had a body. Her body wrought a transformation and she was born. Now there is yet another transformation and she is dead. She is like the four seasons in the way that spring, summer, autumn and winter follow each other. She is now at peace, lying in her chamber, but if I were to sob and cry it would certainly appear that I could not comprehend the ways of destiny. This is why I stopped.'

[. . .]

Chuang Tzu said, 'An archer, not bothering to take aim, by sheer luck hits the centre of the target. We could call him a good archer, but in that case, everyone in the world could be called a Yi the Archer, isn't that right?'

'OK,' said Hui Tzu.

Chuang Tzu said, 'People differ over what they consider to be right, but everyone knows what they think is right. So everyone in the world could be called a Yao, isn't that right?'

'OK,' said Hui Tzu.

Chuang Tzu said, 'So, there are four schools – the Literati, Mohists, Yangists and Pingists – which along with your own, Sir, make five. So which of these is right? Perhaps it is more like the case of Lu Chu? One of his followers said, "I have taken hold of your Tao, Master, and I can heat the pot in winter and make ice in summer." Lu Chu said, "But this is surely just using yang for yang and yin for yin. This is not what I would call the Tao. I will show you my Tao." So he tuned up two lutes and put one in the hall and the other in a private apartment. On striking the note Kung on one, the Kung note vibrated on the other. Likewise with the Chueh note, for the instruments were in harmony. Then he re-tuned one so that it was not in harmony with any of the five key notes. When this was played, all twenty-five of the strings on the other one vibrated, all faithful to their own note and all set off by the one note on the other lute. So, if you insist you are right, aren't you like this?'

Hui Tzi replied, 'The followers of Confucius, Mo, Yang and Ping, like to tackle me in debate, each one trying to defeat the other, each violently trying to shout me down with their various arguments – but they haven't succeeded yet. So what about that?'

Chuang Tzu said, 'A citizen of Chi, not concerned by any mutilation, sold his son to someone in Sung, where he became a gatekeeper. Yet this same man would go to great lengths to protect any of his bells or chimes. But he would not go looking for his son beyond the borders of his own country, such was his understanding of what is worthwhile! Or what if that well-known character, the citizen of Chu who was maimed and a gatekeeper, at midnight in another country, were to pick a fight with a boatman? Then he would never get across the river and would only have provoked the boatman's anger.'

[. . .]

Hui Tzu argued with Chuang Tzu and said, 'What you say is useless!'

'You have to understand what is useless, then you can talk about what is useful,' said Chuang Tzu. 'Heaven and Earth are vast indeed and yet human beings only use the tiny part of the universe on which they tread. However, if you dug away beneath your feet until you came to the Yellow Springs, could anyone make use of this?'

'Useless,' said Hui Tzu.

'So indeed it is true that what is useless is clearly useful,' said Chuang Tzu.

Chuang Tzu continued, 'If someone has the itch to travel, what can stop him? But if someone does not wish to travel, then what can make him? The one who hides in conformity or the one who is distant and seeks oblivion, both fail to achieve perfect understanding and Virtue! They stumble and fall but do not recover. They crash ahead like fire and never look back. Even if they are a ruler with ministers, this too passes. These titles change with each generation and neither is better than the other. It is said that the perfect man leaves no trace of his actions.

'To respect the past and despise the present, this is

what scholars do. Even the followers of Chi Hsi Wei, who view this generation in that way, are swept along without choice. Only the perfect man is able to be in the world and not become partisan, can follow others and not get lost. He does not absorb their teachings, he just listens and understands without any commitment.

'The eye that is penetrating can see clearly;
the ear that is acute hears well;
the nose that discriminates distinguishes smells;
the mouth with a keen sense of taste enjoys
    the flavours;
the heart that feels deeply has wisdom
and the wisdom that cuts to the quick is Virtue.

'Through all that is, the Tao will not be blocked, for if it is blocked, it gasps, and if it gasps, chaos breaks through. Chaos destroys the life in all. Everything that lives does so through breath. However, if breath will not come, this cannot be blamed on Heaven. Heaven seeks to course breath through the body day in and day out without ceasing: it is humanity which impedes this. The womb has its chambers and the heart has its Heavenly journey. However, if rooms are not large enough, then mother-in-law and wife will argue. If the heart does not wander in Heaven, then the six openings of sensation will compete with each other. The great forests, the hills and mountains surpass humanity in their spirit because they cannot be overcome.

'Virtue overflows into fame and desire for fame overflows into excess. Plans arise from a crisis and knowledge comes through argument. Obstinacy fuels resolution and official actions arise from the desires of all. When spring comes, the rains come along with the sunshine, the plants surge into life and harvesting tools are made ready again. Half of all that has fallen begins to sprout, and no one knows why for sure.

'Quietude and silence are healing for those who are ill;
massage is beneficial to the old;
peaceful contemplation can calm the distressed.
To be sure, it is only the disturbed person who
   needs these.
Someone who is at ease and is untroubled by
   such things has no need of this.
The sage reforms everything below Heaven, but
   the spiritual man does not enquire how.
The worthy person improves his generation, –
   but the sage does not enquire how.
The ruler governs the country, but the worthy
   person does not enquire how.
The petty man makes do in these times, but the
   ruler does not enquire how.

'The gatekeeper of Yen Gate had a father who died and the gatekeeper was praised for the extremities of self-deprivation he inflicted on himself, and was honoured by the title of Model Officer. Some others in the area also underwent such extremities, and half of them died. Yao offered the country to Hsu Yu and Hsu Yu fled from him. Tang offered the kingdom to Wu Kuang and Wu Kuang became angry. Chi To heard this and retreated with his followers to the waters of the Kuan, where the local nobles came and commiserated with him for three years. For the same reason, Shen Tu Ti threw himself into the Yellow River. A fish trap is used to catch fish, but once the fish have been taken, the trap is forgotten. The rabbit trap is used to snare rabbits, but once the rabbit is captured, the trap is ignored. Words are used to express concepts, but once you have grasped the concepts, the words are forgotten. I would like to find someone who has forgotten the words so I could debate with such a person!'

[. . .]

Chuang Tzu was following a funeral when he passed by the grave of Hui Tzu. He looked round at those following him and said, 'The man of Ying had on the end of his nose a piece of mud as small as a fly's wing. He sent for the craftsman Shih to cut it off. Shih swirled his axe around and swept it down, creating such a wind as it rushed past that it removed all trace of the mud from the man of Ying, who stood firm, not at all worried. The ruler Yuan of Sung heard of this and called craftsman Shih to visit him.

' "Would you be so kind as to do this for me?" he said.

'Craftsman Shih replied, "Your servant was indeed once able to work like that, but the type of material I worked upon is long since dead."

'Since the Master has died, I have not had any suitable material to work upon. I have no one I can talk with any longer.'

PART 6

Horses' Hooves

Horses have hooves so that their feet can grip on frost and snow, and hair so that they can withstand the wind and cold. They eat grass and drink water, they buck and gallop, for this is the innate nature of horses. Even if they had great towers and magnificent halls, they would not be interested in them. However, when Po Lo came on the scene, he said, 'I know how to train horses.' He branded them, cut their hair and their hooves, put halters on their heads, bridled them, hobbled them and shut them up in stables. Out of ten horses at least two or three die. Then he makes them hungry and thirsty, gallops them, races them, parades them, runs them together. He keeps before them the fear of the bit and ropes, behind them the fear of the whip and crop. Now more than half the horses are dead.

The potter said, 'I know how to use clay, how to mould it into rounds like the compass and into squares as though I had used a T-square.' The carpenter said, 'I know how to use wood: to make it bend, I use the template; to make it straight, I use the plumb line.' However, is it really the innate nature of clay and wood to be moulded by compass and T-square, template and plumb line? It is true, nevertheless, that generation after generation has said, 'Po Lo is good at controlling horses, and indeed the potter and carpenter are good with clay and wood.' And the same nonsense is spouted by those who rule the world.

I think that someone who truly knows how to rule the world would not be like this. The people have a true nature, they weave their cloth, they farm to produce food. This is their basic Virtue. They are all one in this, not separated, and it is from Heaven. Thus, in an age of perfect Virtue the people walk slowly and solemnly. They see straight and true. In times such as these the mountains have neither paths nor tunnels, on the lakes there are neither boats nor bridges; all life lives with its own kind, living close together. The birds and beasts multiply in their flocks and herds, the grass and trees grow tall. It is true that at such a time the birds and beasts can be led around without ropes, and birds' nests can be seen with ease.

In this time of perfect Virtue, people live side by side with the birds and beasts, sharing the world in common with all life. No one knows of distinctions such as nobles and the peasantry! Totally without wisdom but with virtue which does not disappear; totally without desire they are known as truly simple. If people are truly simple, they can follow their true nature. Then the perfect sage comes, going on about benevolence, straining for self-righteousness, and suddenly everyone begins to have doubts. They start to fuss over the music, cutting and trimming the rituals, and thus the whole world is disturbed. If the pure essence had not been so cut about, how could they have otherwise ended up with sacrificial bowls? If the raw jade was not broken apart, how could the symbols of power be made? If the Tao and Te – Way and Virtue – had not been ignored, how could benevolence and righteousness have been preferred? If innate nature had not been left behind, how could rituals and music have been invented? If the five colours had not been confused, how could patterns and designs have occurred? If the five notes had not been confused, how could they have been supplanted by the six tones? The abuse of the true elements to make artefacts was the crime of the craftsman. The abuse of the Tao and Te – Way and Virtue – to make benevolence and righteousness, this was the error of the sage.

Horses, when they live wild, eat grass and drink water; when they are content, they entwine their necks and rub each other. When angry, they turn their backs on each other and kick out. This is what horses know. But if harnessed together and lined up under constraints, they know to look sideways and to arch their necks, to career around and try to spit out the bit and rid themselves of the reins. The knowledge thus gained by the horse, and its wicked behaviour, is in fact the fault of Po Lo.

PART 7

What's the Point of a Great Deal of Knowledge?

A great deal of knowledge is needed to make bows, cross-bows, nets, arrows and so forth, but the result is that the birds fly higher in distress. A great deal of knowledge is needed to make fishing lines, traps, baits and hooks, but the result is that the fish disperse in distress in the water. A great deal of knowledge is needed to make traps, snares and nets, but the result is that the animals are disturbed and seek refuge in marshy lands. In the same way, the versatility needed to produce rhetoric, to plot and scheme, spread rumours and debate pointlessly, to dust off arguments and seek apparent agreement, is also considerable, but the result is that the people are confused. So everything under Heaven is in a state of distress, all because of the pursuit of knowledge. Everything in the world knows how to seek for knowledge that they do not have, but do not know how to find what they already know. Everything in the world knows how to condemn what they dislike, but do not know how to condemn what they have which is wrong. This is what causes such immense confusion. It is as if the brightness of the sun and moon had been eclipsed above, while down below the hills and streams have lost their power, as though the natural flow of the four seasons had been broken. There is no humble insect, not even any plant, that has not lost its innate nature. This is the consequence for the world of seeking after knowledge. From the Three Dynasties down to the present day it has been like this. The good and honest people are ignored, while spineless flatterers are advanced. The quiet and calm of actionless action is cast aside and pleasure is taken in argument. It is this nonsense which has caused such confusion for everything under Heaven.

[. . .]

Are people too cheerful? If so, they harm the yang. Are people too vengeful? If so, they harm the yin. If both yin and yang are corrupted, then the four seasons will not follow each other, the balance of hot and cold will not be kept and this results in distress to the very bodies of the people! People will be unable to control a balance between joy and anger. It makes them restless, moving here, moving there, plotting to no purpose, travelling for no good reason or result. The consequence of this is that the world becomes concerned with mighty goals and plots, ambition and hatred, which brings in its wake the likes of Robber Chih, Tseng and Shih. As a result, the world may wish to reward the good, but there are not enough rewards available; nor can it adequately punish the bad, for there are not enough punishments.

[. . .]

So it is that the noble master who finds he has to follow some course to govern the world will realize that actionless action is the best course. By non-action, he can rest in the real substance of his nature and destiny. If he appreciates his own body as he appreciates the world, then the world can be placed in his care. He who loves his body as he loves the world can be trusted to govern the world. If the noble master can prevent his five main organs from being destroyed, and his vision and hearing also; if he can become as lifeless as a corpse and develop his dragon powers; if he can thus still himself, his words will sound like thunder while his actions will be seen as the actions of a spirit from Heaven, who is guided by Heaven. If he is unconcerned and engaged in actionless action, his gentle spirit will draw all life to him like a dust cloud. How then would such a person have time for governing the world?

[. . .]

Yun Chiang was travelling east, carried along upon the wings of a whirlwind. Suddenly he met Hung Mung, who was jumping around, slapping his thighs and hopping like a bird. Yun Chiang saw this and stopped dead, standing still in respect, and said, 'Elderly man, who are you? What are you doing?'

Hung Mung continued to slap his thighs and hop like a bird, then replied, 'Enjoying myself!'

Yun Chiang said, 'I would like to ask a question.'

Hung Mung looked at Yun Chiang and said, 'That's a shame!'

Yun Chiang said, 'The very breath of Heaven is no longer in harmony. Earth's very breath is ensnared, the six breaths do not mix, the four seasons do not follow each other. Now I want to combine the six breaths in order to bring life to all things. How do I do this?'

Hung Mung slapped his thighs, hopped around and said, 'I don't know, I don't know!'

Yun Chiang could go no further with this questioning. But three years later, travelling east, he passed the wilderness of Sung and came upon Hung Mung again. Yun Chiang, very pleased, rushed towards him, stood before him and said, 'Heaven, have you forgotten me? Heaven, have you forgotten me?' Bowing his head twice, he asked for teaching from Hung Mung.

Hung Mung said, 'Wandering everywhere, without a clue why. Wildly impulsive, without a clue where. I wander around in this odd fashion, I see that nothing comes without reason. What can I know?'

Yun Chiang replied, 'I am also wildly impulsive, but the people follow me wherever I am. I cannot stop them following me. Now, because they follow me, I want to have a word of teaching from you.'

'The disruption of the ways of Heaven distresses the true being of things, halting the fulfilment of Heaven's Mysteries,' said Hung Mung. 'This causes the animals to disperse, the birds to sing throughout the night, misfortune to hit the crops and the woods, and disaster to blight the very insects themselves. Alas, all this is caused by the people's error of thinking they know how to rule!'

'What should I do then?' said Yun Chiang.

'Oh, you distress them! Like a spirit, a spirit I will dance away,' said Hung Mung.

'I have had such trouble meeting you,' said Yun Chiang. 'Oh Heaven, just give me one other word.'

'Oh ho!' said Hung Mung. 'Strengthen your heart. Remain sure in actionless action, and all things will then transform themselves. Reject your body, throw out hearing and eyesight, forget that you are anyone, become one with the Vast and the Void. Loosen the heart, free the spirit, be calm as if without a soul. All living things return to their root, return to their root, not knowing why. Constantly in darkness, constantly in darkness, and throughout their physical existence they never depart from this. If they tried to understand this, they would depart from this. Ask not for its name, seek not for its shape. So all life comes to birth through itself.'

Yun Chiang replied, 'Heaven, you have honoured me with this Virtue, taught me through Mystery; my whole life I sought it, now I have it.' He bowed his head twice and got up. He said farewell and left.

PART 8

The Action of Non-action is Called Heaven

So the sages contemplate Heaven but do not assist it.
They are concerned to perfect their Virtue but do
not allow it to encumber them.
They set forth according to the Tao but do not
make plans.
They work with benevolence but put no reliance
upon it.
They draw extensively upon righteousness but do
not try to build it up.
They observe the rituals but do not set great store
by them.
They do what they have to and never shirk their
responsibilities.
They try to make their laws applicable but do
not believe them effective.
They value the people and do not take them
for granted.
They make use of things and do not dismiss
them lightly.
True, things are worthless but they must be used.
Those who do not see Heaven clearly will not
be pure in Virtue.
Those who fail to follow the Tao cannot follow
any other path.
What a disaster for those who cannot follow the Tao!

What is this Tao?
There is the Tao of Heaven;
there is the Tao of humanity.
Non-action brings respect: this is Heaven's Tao.
To be active is the Tao of humanity.
It is Heaven's Tao that is the ruler;
the Tao of humanity is the servant.
The Tao of Heaven and the Tao of humanity are
  poles apart.
Do not fail to reflect upon this.
[. . .]
Heaven and Earth are vast,
and their diversity comes from one source.
Although there are ten thousand forms of life,
they are one in their order.
Human beings are multitudinous,
but they are governed by one ruler.
The ruler is rooted in Virtue and perfected by Heaven.
It is said that long ago
the rulers of everything below Heaven
ruled through actionless action,
through Heavenly Virtue and nothing else.
[. . .]
The action of non-action is called Heaven.
The words of non-action are called Virtue.
To love all humanity and to bring success to them
  is called benevolence.
To unite that which is not united is called greatness.
To go beyond barriers and boundaries is called
  open-handedness.
To have a vast multitude of diverse things is called wealth.

To have and to hold Virtue is called guidance.
To grow in maturity in Virtue is called stability
To be aligned with the Tao is called completion.
To refuse to allow anything external which distracts
    you is called perfection.

The nobleman who clearly perceives these ten things
will be also magnanimous in his ventures and his actions
will benefit all life.

Such a man will leave the gold in the mountain
and the pearls to lie in the deep.
He does not view money and goods as true profit,
nor is he attracted by fame and fortune,
nor by enjoyment of long life,
nor sadness at an early death;
he does not value wealth as a blessing,
nor is he ashamed by poverty.
He will not lust for the wealth of a generation to
    have as his own;
he has no wish to rule the whole world as his
    private domain.
His honour is clarity of understanding that all
    life is part of one treasury
and that death and birth are united.

The Sage Master said,

'The Tao, how deep and quiet it lies;
how pure is its clarity!
Without it neither gold nor stone would resonate.

The gold and stones have sounds within them
but if they are not struck, then no sound comes forth.
All the multitudinous creatures have dimensions
    beyond calculation!

[. . .]

'The way sages rule?' said Chun Mang. 'Only appoint those who are fit for the office; make appointments in accordance with the worthiness of those appointed; act only after studying the situation thoroughly. When deeds and words are in accord, the whole world is transformed. Consequently, a wave of the hand or a sharp look will bring the peoples of all the world rushing to you. This is the way sages rule.'

'Can I ask about the Virtuous ones?'

'The Virtuous one is still and without thought:
when he moves he is without design;
he keeps no tally of right and wrong, good or bad.
Virtuous ones share their gains with all within
    the four seas
and from this they derive pleasure.
They share what they have and are content.
Mournful, they are like a child who has lost
    his mother;
uncertain, they are like travellers who are lost.
Though blessed with great wealth and comforts,
they have no idea where it comes from;
they have more than enough to eat and drink,
but have no idea where it comes from.
This is the style of Virtuous ones.'

'What about the spiritual ones?'

Chun Mang said,

'Their spirits rise up to the brightest light
and their bodies disappear.
They are gloriously enraptured.
They live out their fate,
The spiritual one pursues to its end what is truly him
and dwells in the delight of Heaven and Earth
while his multitudinous cares fall away.
All things return to their true nature.
This is called Primal Mystery.'
[. . .]
It is Heaven's Tao to journey and to gather
      no moss,
thus all the forms of life are brought to perfection.
It is the Emperor's Tao to journey and to gather
      no moss,
which is why the whole world comes to his feet.
It is the sages' Tao to journey and to gather
      no moss,
thus all that lies within the oceans venerates them.
To understand Heaven clearly,
to comprehend the sages,
to journey through the entire cosmos
following the Virtue of the Emperors and the kings
but also to be spontaneous themselves:
this is the nature of those who comprehend,
seeming not to know
but being centred in stillness.

The sages are quiescent, not because of any value in being quiescent, they simply are still. Not even the multitude of beings can disturb them, so they are calm. Water, when it is still, reflects back even your eyebrows and beard. It is perfectly level and from this the carpenter takes his level. If water stilled offers such clarity, imagine what pure spirit offers! The sage's heart is stilled! Heaven and Earth are reflected in it, the mirror of all life. Empty, still, calm, plain, quiet, silent, non-active, this is the centredness of Heaven and Earth and of the Tao and of Virtue. The Emperor, king, and sages rest there. Resting, they are empty; empty, they can be full; fullness is fulfilment. From the empty comes stillness; in stillness they can travel; in travelling they achieve. In stillness they take actionless action. Through actionless action they expect results from those with responsibilities. Through actionless action they are happy, very happy; being so happy they are not afflicted by cares and worries, for these have no place, and their years of life are prolonged. Empty, still, calm, plain, quiet, silent, actionless action is the foundation of all life. If you are clear on this and facing south, it means you are a noble like Yao; if you are clear on this and facing north, you will become a minister like Shun.

[. . .]

Chuang Tzu said,

'My Master Teacher! My Master Teacher!
He judges all life but does not feel he is being
     judgemental;
he is generous to multitudes of generations
but does not think this benevolent;
he is older than the oldest

but he does not think himself old;
he overarches Heaven and sustains Earth,
shaping and creating endless bodies
but he does not think himself skilful.
This is what is known as Heavenly happiness.

'There is a saying: "If you know the happiness of
Heaven, then you know that life is from Heaven and death
is the transformation of things. In their stillness they
are yin and in their journeying they are yang." To know
Heavenly happiness means that you do not upset Heaven,
nor go against others. You are not reliant on material
things, you are not rebuked by the ghosts. There is a saying: "He moves with Heaven and rests with Earth, his
heart is one, he is the king of the whole world; the ghosts
do not worry him and his soul is not wearied, his heart is one
with all living beings." This means his emptiness and stillness enter all beings in Heaven and Earth, travelling along-
side all beings. This is known as the Heavenly happiness.
Heavenly happiness is the heart of the sage; this is how he
cares for all under Heaven.'

The Virtue of emperors and kings considers Heaven
and Earth as its parents, the Tao and Virtue as its master
and actionless action as its core. Through actionless
action they can make the whole world do as they will and
yet not be wearied. Through action they cannot even
begin to fulfil what the world requires. This is why the
ancient ones valued actionless action.

[. . .]

Thus the ancient kings of the world, who knew everything about Heaven and Earth, had no designs; even

though they understood the whole of life, they did not
speak out; though their skills were greater than any in
the lands bounded by oceans, they did nothing.

Heaven produces nothing,
yet all life is transformed;
Earth does not support,
yet all life is sustained;
the Emperor and the king take actionless action,
yet the whole world is served.
There is a saying that there is
nothing as spiritual as Heaven,
nothing as rich as Earth,
nothing as great as emperors and kings.

[. . .]

Thus it was that the ancient ones clearly grasped the
great Tao, seeking first the meaning of Heaven and then
the meaning of its Tao and Virtue.

When they clearly understood the Tao and Virtue,
they then understood benevolence and righteousness.
When they clearly grasped benevolence and
    righteousness,
they could see how to perform their duties.
When they grasped how to perform their duties,
they came to understand form and fame.
When they comprehended form and fame,
they were able to make appointments.
When they had made appointments,

they went on to examining people and their efforts.
When they had examined people's efforts,
they moved to judgements of good or bad.
When they had made judgements of good
    and bad,
they went on to punishments and rewards.

[. . .]

In days gone by Shun spoke to Yao, saying, 'Being Heaven's king, how do you use your heart?'

'I do not abuse those who are defenceless,' said Yao, 'nor do I ignore the poor. I mourn for those who die, caring for the orphaned child and for the widow. This is how I use my heart.'

'Righteous as far as righteousness goes, but not that great,' commented Shun.

'What ought I to do, then?' said Yao.

'When Heaven's Virtue is found, the hills rejoice, the sun and moon shine and the four seasons are in line. The regular pattern of each day and night follows properly and the rain clouds are moved accordingly.'

Yao said, 'So all I've really been doing is getting worked up and bothered! You seek compliance with Heaven, whereas I have sought compliance with humanity.'

[. . .]

Confucius travelled west to place his books in the archives of Chou. Tzu Lu offered advice, saying, 'I have heard that the official in charge of the Royal Archives is Lao Tzu.

But he has resigned and lives at home. Sir, if you want to place your books there, go and see him and ask his assistance.'

'Splendid,' said Confucius. So off he went to see Lao Tzu, but Lao Tzu refused to help. So Confucius took out his Twelve Classics, and started to preach.

When he was halfway through, Lao Tzu said, 'This is too much. Put it briefly.'

Confucius said, 'In essence, it is benevolence and righteousness.'

'May I ask,' said Lao Tzu, 'are benevolence and righteousness of the very essence of humanity?'

'Certainly,' said Confucius. 'If the nobleman is without benevolence, he has no purpose; if without righteousness, he has no life. Benevolence and righteousness, these are truly of the innate nature of humanity. How else could it be?'

'May I ask, what are benevolence and righteousness?'

'To be at one, centred in one's heart, in love with all, without selfishness, this is what benevolence and righteousness are,' replied Confucius.

'Really! Your words reveal misunderstanding,' said Lao Tzu. ' "Love of all", that's both vague and an exaggeration! "Without selfishness", isn't that rather selfish? Sir, if you want people to remain simple, shouldn't you look to the ways of Heaven and Earth?

'Heaven and Earth have their boundaries which
    are constant;
the sun and moon hold their courses in their
    brightness;

80

the stars and planets proceed in the boundaries
    of their order;
the birds and creatures find their confines within
    their herds and flocks.
Think of the trees which stand within their own
    boundaries in order.

'So Sir, walk with Virtue and travel with the Tao, and you will reach the perfect end. Why bother with all this benevolence and righteousness, prancing along as if you were beating a drum and looking for a lost child? Sir, you will just confuse people's true nature!'

[. . .]

The Master said,

'The Tao does not hesitate before that which is vast,
nor does it abandon the small.
Thus it is that all life is enlivened by it.
So immense, so immense there is nothing which
    is not held by it;
so deep, so unfathomable beyond any reckoning.
The form of its Virtue is in benevolence and
    righteousness,
though this is a minor aspect of its spirit.
Who but the perfect man could comprehend all this?
The perfect man has charge of this age,
a somewhat daunting task!
However, this does not fool him or trap him.
He holds the reins of power over the whole world

but it is of little consequence to him.
His discernment unearths all falsehood
but he gives no thought to personal gain.
He gets to the heart of issues and knows how to
    protect the foundation of truth.
Thus Heaven and Earth are outside him,
he ignores all life and his spirit is never wearied.
He travels with the Tao,
is in agreement with Virtue,
    bids farewell to benevolence and righteousness
    and ignores ritual and music,
    because the perfect man has set his heart upon
        what is right.'

This generation believes that the value of the Tao is to be found in books. But books are nothing more than words, and words have value but only in terms of their meaning. Meaning is constantly seeking to express what cannot be said in words and thus passed on. This generation values words and puts them into books, yet what it values is perhaps mistaken, because what it values is not really all that valuable. So we look at things and see things, but it is only an outward form and colour, and what can be heard is just the name and sound. How sad that this generation imagines that the form, colour, name and sound are enough to capture the essence of something! The form, colour, name and sound are in no way sufficient to capture or convey the truth, which is why it is said that the knowledgeable do not speak and those who speak are not knowledgeable. But how can this generation understand this?

PART 9

Does Heaven Move?

Does Heaven move?
Does the Earth stand still?
Do the sun and moon argue about
    where to go?
Who is lord over all this?
Who binds and controls it?
Who, doing nothing, makes all of this be?
Is there some hidden cause that makes things
    as they are, whether they wish or not?
Or is it just that everything moves and turns
    because it has no choice?
Do the clouds come before the rain, or does
    the rain cause the clouds?
What causes them to be?
Who, doing nothing, brings all this joyful
    excess into being?
The winds come from the north,
going first to west then to east,
swirling up on high, to go who knows where?
Whose breath are they?
Who, doing nothing, creates all this activity?

[. . .]

Duke Huan was sitting up in his hall reading a book. The

wheelwright Pien was down below in the courtyard making a wheel. He put down his chisel and hammer, went up to the hall and asked Duke Huan, 'May I ask you, Sir, what words you are reading?'

Duke Huan replied, 'The words of the sages.'

'Are these sages still living?'

'They are long dead,' said Duke Huan.

'Then, Sir, what you are reading is nothing but rubbish left over from these ancient men!'

'How dare you, a wheelwright, comment on what I read! If you can explain this, fine, if not you shall die!' thundered Duke Huan.

The wheelwright Pien replied, 'Your Lordship's servant looks at it from the perspective of his own work. When I work on a wheel, if I hit too softly, pleasant as this is, it doesn't make for a good wheel. If I hit furiously, I get tired and the thing doesn't work! So, not too soft, not too vigorous, I grasp it in my hand and hold it in my heart. I cannot express this by word of mouth, I just know it. I cannot teach this to my son, nor can my son learn it from me. So for seventy years I have gone along this path and here I am still making wheels. The ancient ones, when they died, took their words with them. Which is why I can state that what Your Lordship is reading is nothing more than rubbish left over from these ancient ones!'

[. . .]

Confucius had pottered along for fifty-one years and had never heard anyone speak of the Tao until he went south to Pei and went to see Lao Tzu.

Lao Tzu said, 'So you've come then, Sir? I have heard of you, that you are the wise man of the north. Have you, Sir, followed the Tao?'

'I have not yet followed it,' replied Confucius.

'Well, Sir, where have you looked?'

'I looked for it in what can be measured and regulated but even after five years I still haven't been able to find it.'

'So, Sir, what did you do then?' asked Lao Tzu.

'I looked for it in yin and yang, but ten, twelve years went by and I still couldn't find it.'

'Obviously!' said Lao Tzu. 'If the Tao could be served up, everyone would serve it up to their lords. If the Tao could be offered, there is no one who would not offer it to their parents. If the Tao could be spoken of, there is no one who would not speak of it to their brothers and sisters. If the Tao could be passed on, there is no one who would not pass it on to their heirs. However, it obviously cannot be so and the reason is as follows.

> 'If there is no true centre within to receive it,
> it cannot remain;
> if there is no true direction outside to guide it,
> it cannot be received.
> If the true centre is not brought out
> it cannot receive on the outside.
> The sage cannot draw it forth.
> If what comes in from the outside is not welcomed
>   by the true centre,
> then the sage cannot let it go.

[. . .]

Confucius went to see Lao Tzu and talked with him about benevolence and righteousness. Lao Tzu said, 'If you get grit in your eye from winnowing chaff, then Heaven and Earth and the four directions get mixed up. A mosquito or gadfly which stings you can keep you awake all night. And benevolence and righteousness, when forced upon us, disturb your heart and produce great distress. You, Sir, if you want to stop everything below Heaven losing its original simplicity, you must travel with the wind and stand firm in Virtue. Why do you exert yourself so much, banging a big drum and hunting for a lost child? The snow goose doesn't need a daily bath to stay white, nor does the crow need to be stained every day to stay black. Black and white comes from natural simplicity, not from argument. Fame and fortune, though sought after, do not make people greater than they actually are. When the waters dry up and the fish are stranded on the dry land, they huddle together and try to keep each other moist by spitting and wetting each other. But wouldn't it be even better if they could just forget each other, safe in their lakes and rivers?'

After seeing Lao Tzu, Confucius went home and for three days he said nothing. His followers asked him, 'Master, now you have seen Lao Tzu, what do you make of him?'

'I have now seen a dragon!' said Confucius. 'A dragon coils up to show its form, it stretches out to display its power. It rides upon the breath of the clouds and is nourished by yin and yang. My mouth gaped open and I could not shut it. What can I say about Lao Tzu?'

[. . .]

The ancient ones talked of the Timeliness of Purpose, but they did not mean having official carriages and badges of office. They simply meant that it was happiness so complete as to need nothing more. Today what is called Timeliness of Purpose means having official carriages and badges of office. Carriages and badges are of the body, they do not touch the innate nature. From time to time such benefits may come. When this happens, you cannot help it, no more than you can stop them going again. So having carriages and badges of office is no reason for becoming proud and arrogant in our purposes, nor are distress and poverty any reason for becoming vulgar. View both conditions as one and the same, so be free from anxiety and leave it at that. So if loss of what gives happiness causes you distress when it fades, you can now understand that such happiness is worthless. It is said, those who lose themselves in their desire for things also lose their innate nature by being vulgar. They are known as people who turn things upside down.

PART 10

Reality and Happiness

The season of the autumn floods had come and the hundred rivers were pouring into the Yellow River. The waters were churning and so wide that, looking across from one bank to the other, it was impossible to distinguish an ox from a horse. At this the Lord of the Yellow River was decidedly pleased, thinking that the most beautiful thing in the whole world belonged to him. Flowing with the river, he travelled east until he came at last to the North Ocean, where he looked east and could see no end to the waters. He shook his head, the Lord of the Yellow River, and looked out to confront Jo, god of the Ocean, sighing and saying.

'The folk proverb says, "The person who has heard of the Tao a hundred times thinks he is better than anyone else." This refers to me. I have heard people mock the scholarship of the Confucians and give scant regard to the righteousness of Po Yi, but I didn't believe them. Now I have seen your endless vastness. If I had not come to your gate, I would have been in danger, and been mocked by those of the Great Method.'

Jo of the North Ocean replied, 'A frog in a well cannot discuss the ocean, because he is limited by the size of his well. A summer insect cannot discuss ice, because it knows only its own season. A narrow-minded scholar cannot discuss the Tao, because he is constrained by his teachings. Now you have come out of your banks and seen the Great Ocean. You now know your own inferiority, so it is now possible to discuss great principles with you. Under Heaven there are no greater waters than the ocean. Ten thousand rivers flow into it, and it has never been known to stop, but it never fills. At Wei Lu the water disappears but the ocean never empties. Spring and autumn bring no changes. It pays no attention to floods or droughts. It is so much more than the waters of the Yangtze and the Yellow Rivers, it is impossible to estimate. However, I have never made much of this. I just compare myself with Heaven and Earth and my life-breath I receive from yin and yang. I am just a little stone or a little tree set on a great hill, in comparison to Heaven and Earth. As I perceive my own inferiority, how could I ever be proud?

'To compare all the space filled by the four oceans, is it not like a pile of stones beside a marsh in comparison with the vastness between Heaven and Earth? To compare China with all the space between the oceans, is it not like one single piece of grain in a granary? When talking of all life, we count them in tens of thousands, and humanity is just one of them. People inhabit the Nine Provinces, but humanity is just one portion of all the life that is sustained by grain, wherever carriages or boats can go. In comparison to all the multitudinous forms of life, isn't humanity like just a single hair on a horse?

[. . .]

The Lord of the Yellow River said, 'The debaters of this generation say, "The tiniest thing has no body, the most enormous thing cannot be contained." Are these words true?'

Jo of the North Ocean replied, 'From the viewpoint of the tiniest, we look at what is so enormous and we cannot comprehend it. From the viewpoint of the most enormous, we look at what is tiniest and we cannot see it clearly. The tiniest is the smallest of the small, the biggest is the largest of the large; so we must distinguish between them, even though this is just a matter of circumstance. However, both the coarse and the refined have form. Without any form, there is no way to enumerate them. What can be said in words is the coarseness of things; what can be grasped through ideas is the subtlety of things. But words cannot describe nor ideas grasp, and this has nothing to do with coarseness or refinement.

'So it is that the great man through his actions will not set out to harm others, nor make much of benevolence and charity; he does not make any move for gain, nor consider the servant at the gate as lowly; he will not barter for property and riches, nor does he make much of his having turned them down; he asks for no one's help, nor does he make much of his own self-reliance, nor despise the greedy and mean; he does not follow the crowd, nor does he make much of being so different; he comes behind the crowd, but does not make much of those who get ahead through flattery. The titles and honours of this world are of no interest to him, nor is he concerned at the disgrace of punishments. He knows there is no distinction between right and wrong, nor between great and little. I have heard it said, "The Tao man earns no reputation, perfect Virtue is not followed, the great man is self-less." In perfection, this is the path he follows.'

The Lord of the Yellow River asked, 'Whether they are external or internal, how come we have these distinctions between noble and mean? Why do we distinguish between small and great?'

'Viewed from the perspective of the Tao,' said Jo of the North Ocean, 'things are neither elevated nor lowly. Viewed from the perspective of things, each one considers itself as elevated and the rest as lowly. Viewed from the perspective of the everyday opinion, neither elevation nor lowliness is to be understood from the perspective of individual things. Taking into account differing views, something which is seen as big because it is big means that, in all the multitudes of life, everything can be viewed as big. Likewise, if something is seen as small because it is small, then all forms of life can be viewed as small. If we know that Heaven and Earth are as tiny as a grain or the tip of a hair is as vast as a mountain range, then we will have grasped that our understanding of size is relative. In terms of what each does, we view something as useful because it is useful, which means that, in all the multitudes of life, everything can be viewed as useful. In the same way, if something is viewed as useless because it appears useless, then all forms of life can be viewed as useless. If we know that east and west are opposite each other, but also need each other, then we can understand how mutual exchange and interaction work. Viewed from the perspective of choice, if something is seen as good because it undoubtedly is good, then in all the multitudes of life there is nothing which is not good. Likewise, if something is viewed as wrong because it undoubtedly is wrong, then there is no form of life which cannot be viewed as wrong.'

[. . .]

'Be quiet, be quiet, Lord of the Yellow River! How could you know anything about the gateway to nobility or meanness or the dwelling place of greatness or pettiness?'

'All right then,' said the Lord of the Yellow River. 'What am I to do and what may I not do? How can I decide what is worth keeping or rejecting and what is worth going for or leaving?'

Jo of the North Ocean said, 'Viewed from the perspective of the Tao, what is noble and what is mean are both just ceaseless changes. Don't cling to your own ideas, for this is contrary to the greatness of the Tao. What is little and what is much, these are terms of very limited use. Do not try to be just One, this just highlights how far away you are from the Tao. Be stern and strict like a ruler of a country who favours no one. Be gentle, be gentle like the local earth god to whom offerings are made and who does not grant fortune selfishly. Be open like air, like the four compass points shed light but do not permit boundaries. If you lovingly tend all forms of life, how could you favour one? This is known as being impartial. Consider all life as unified and then how could you talk in terms of long or short? The Tao has neither beginning nor end, but all living things have both death and birth, so you cannot be sure of them. One moment they are empty, the next moment full. They are unreliable. The years cannot be reversed nor time halted. Decay, maturity, fullness and emptiness, when they end, begin over again. So we can talk of great righteousness, and discuss the fundamental principle within all forms of life. The life force is a headlong gallop, speeding along, changing with every movement and altering every minute. As to what you should and should not do? Just go with this process of change.'

'If this is the case,' said the Lord of the Yellow River, 'then what is so important about the Tao?'

Jo of the North Ocean replied, 'To understand the Tao is to understand the principle. If you understand the principle, you know how to deal with things as they arise. Knowing this, you can ensure that nothing detrimental to yourself occurs. If someone has perfect Virtue, it is not possible for fire to harm, nor for water to drown, nor for either cold or heat to affect, nor birds and beasts to injure him. Not that I say that he dismisses all these things, but that he is able to discriminate between where he is safe and where he is in danger. He is at ease with both calamity and fortune, takes care as to what he approaches or avoids, and therefore nothing harms him. There is a saying that Heaven is internal, humanity external and Virtue comes from the Heavenly. Know Heaven and humanity's actions, root yourself in Heaven and follow Virtue. Then you can bend, stretch, rush forward or hold back, because you will always return to the core and it will be said you have achieved the supreme.'

'But what do you call the Heavenly? What do you call the human?'

Jo of the North Ocean said, 'Oxen have four feet: this is what I call the Heavenly. When horses are harnessed and oxen have pierced noses, this I call the human way. There is the saying. "Don't allow the human to displace the Heavenly," don't allow your intentions to nullify what is ordained. Be careful, guard it and don't lose it, for this is what I call coming back to the True.'

The one-legged creature is envious of the millipede; the millipede is envious of the snake; the snake is envious of the wind; the wind is envious of the eye; the eye is envious of the heart.

The one-legged creature said to the millipede, 'I have one foot that I hop on and I can hardly go anywhere. But you, Sir, have a multitude of feet. How do you manage?'

The millipede said, 'Don't be so certain. Have you never seen someone spit? Out comes a big blob followed by a spray, which falls down like a shower of uncountable drops. Now I just set the Heavenly machinery in motion and as for the rest – I haven't a clue!'

The millipede said to the snake, 'I get about with all these feet, but I can't keep up with you, Sir, who have no feet. Why is this?'

The snake said, 'I am moved by the designs of Heaven, how can I control that? What could I use feet for!'

The snake said to the wind, 'By moving my backbone and ribs, I get along and at least I have some visible form. Now you, Sir, come hurtling along from the North Ocean and disappear off to the South Ocean but without any visible form. How is that?'

The wind said, 'True, I come hurtling along from the North Ocean and disappear off to the South Ocean.

However, it is true that, if you point your finger at me, you are greater than me, or if you stamp on me, you also win. But it is also true that I can bring down great trees and bowl over great houses; only I can do this. Therefore, the one who can overcome all the small problems is in truth the great victor. To have a great victory, why, this is what a sage does.'

[. . .]

Kung Sun Lung asked Mou of Wei, 'When I was younger, I learned the Tao of the earlier kings, and, as I grew up, I saw clearly the significance of benevolence and righteousness. I brought together difference and similarity, discerned hardness and whiteness, what was certain and what was not, what was possible and what was not. I laboured at understanding the Hundred Schools of Philosophy and spoke out against their teachings. I thought I had understanding of all things. Now, however, I have heard the words of Chuang Tzu, and to my surprise I am disturbed by them. Is it that my knowledge is not as good as his, or is it that his understanding is greater? I find I can't even open my mouth, so I ask you what I can do.'

Duke Tzu Mou leaned forward, sighed heavily, looked to Heaven, smiled and said, 'Dear Sir, have you not heard of the frog in the broken-down old well? He said to the turtle of the Eastern Ocean, "I have a great time! I leap on to the well wall, or I go down in the well, stepping along the broken bricks. When I enter the water, I float with it supporting my chin, feet up; on the mud, I dig my feet deep in. I look about me at the larvae, crabs and tadpoles and there is none that is as good as I. To have complete control of the waters of the gorge and not to wish to move but to enjoy the old well, this is great! Dear Sir, why don't you come down and see me sometime?'

'The turtle of the Eastern Ocean tried, but before he had put his left foot into the well, his right knee was stuck. At this he paused, shuffled out backwards and then began to speak about the ocean. "A distance such as a thousand miles doesn't come close to describing its length, nor a depth of a thousand leagues describe its deepness. In the time of Yu, nine years in every ten there were floods, but this did not raise the ocean an inch. In the time of Tang, seven years in every eight there were droughts, but this did not lower the ocean shore an inch. Nothing changes these waters, neither in the short term nor in the long term; they neither recede nor advance, grow larger nor smaller. This is the great happiness of the Eastern Ocean." When the frog in the broken-down old well heard this, he was utterly amazed and astonished; he was utterly astonished, dumbfounded and at a loss.

'For someone whose understanding can't handle such knowledge, such debates about right and wrong, if they persist in trying to see through the words of Chuang Tzu, it is like a mosquito trying to carry a mountain on its back, or a scuttle bug rushing as fast as the Yellow River. This is plainly impossible. For someone whose understanding cannot handle such knowledge, such words of subtlety, all they are capable of is gaining some short-term reward. They are like the frog in the broken-down well, are they not? But Chuang Tzu is not planted firmly in the Yellow Springs of the Underworld, nor leaping, jumping into the stratosphere. There is neither south nor north: he scatters freely to the four points of the compass, and disappears into the depth. There is neither east nor west: starting in the darkest depth, he comes back to the great path. Then you, Sir, you in your astonishment try to sift his views to criticize them, or trawl through them in order to debate. Why, this is like trying to examine Heaven through a narrow tube or using an awl to explore the whole earth. Such tools are too small, aren't they? You, Sir, be on your way! Or possibly, Sir, you have not heard of the young students of Shou Ling and how things went for them in Han Tan? Having not yet learnt the lessons that the people of that country were trying to teach them, they forgot what they had learnt at home, so were reduced to crawling back home. So, Sir, if you don't get out now, you will forget, Sir, what you already knew and fail, Sir, in your career!'

Kung Sun Lung's mouth fell open and would not shut, his tongue stuck to the roof of his mouth and wouldn't drop down, and he shuffled off and ran away.

Chuang Tzu was one day fishing in the Pu river when the King of Chu despatched two senior officials to visit him with a message. The message said, 'I would like to trouble you to administer my lands.'

Chuang Tzu kept a firm grip on his fishing rod and said, 'I hear that in Chu there is a sacred tortoise which died three thousand years ago. The King keeps this in his ancestral temple, wrapped and enclosed. Tell me, would this tortoise have wanted to die and leave his shell to be venerated? Or would he rather have lived and continued to crawl about in the mud?'

The two senior officials said, 'It would rather have lived and continued to crawl about in the mud.'

Chuang Tzu said, 'Shove off, then! I will continue to crawl about in the mud!'

[. . .]

Chuang Tzu and Hui Tzu were walking beside the weir on the River Hao, when Chuang Tzu said, 'Do you see how the fish are coming to the surface and swimming around as they please? That's what fish really enjoy.'

'You're not a fish,' replied Hui Tzu, 'so how can you say you know what fish enjoy?'

Chuang Tzu said: 'You are not me, so how can you know I don't know what fish enjoy?'

Hui Tzu said: 'I am not you, so I definitely don't know what it is you know. However, you are most definitely not a fish and that proves that you don't know what fish really enjoy.'

Chuang Tzu said: 'Ah, but let's return to the original question you raised, if you don't mind. You asked me how I could know what it is that fish really enjoy. Therefore, you already knew I knew it when you asked the question. And I know it by being here on the edge of the River Hao.'

[. . .]

Is it possible anywhere in this whole wide world to have perfect happiness or not? Is there a way to keep yourself alive or not? Now, what can be done and what is to be trusted? What should be avoided and what adhered to?

What should be pursued and what abandoned? Where is happiness and where is evil?

What the whole wide world values is riches, position, long life and fame.

What brings happiness is good times for oneself, fine foods, beautiful clothes, lovely sights and sweet music.

What is despised is poverty, meanness, untimely death and a bad reputation.

What is considered sour is a lifestyle which gives the self no rest, a mouth which never has fine foods, a body without good clothes, eyes that never rest upon lovely views, an ear that never hears sweet music.

Those who cannot get these things become greatly agitated and fearful. This is a foolish way to treat the body!

Those who are wealthy weary themselves dashing around working, getting more and more riches, beyond what they need. The body is treated therefore as just an external thing.

Those in positions of power spend day and night plotting and pondering about what to do. The body is treated in a very careless way. People live their lives, constantly surrounded by anxiety. If they live long before dying, they end up in senility, worn out by concerns: a terrible fate! The body is treated in a very harsh fashion. Courageous men are seen by everyone under Heaven as worthy, but this doesn't preserve them from death. I am not sure I know whether this is sensible or not. Possibly it is, but it does nothing towards saving them. Possibly it is not, but it does save other people. It is said, 'If a friend doesn't listen to the advice you offer him, then bow out and don't argue.' After all, Tzu Hsu argued and lost his life. If he had not argued, he would not be famous. Is it possible that there really is goodness, or not?

Now, when ordinary people attempt to find happiness, I'm not sure whether the happiness found is really happiness or not. I study what ordinary people do to find happiness, what they struggle for, rushing about apparently unable to stop. They say they are happy, but I am not happy and I am not unhappy either. Ultimately, do they have happiness or not? I regard actionless action as worthy of being called happiness, though the ordinary people regard it as a great burden. It is said: 'Perfect happiness is not happiness, perfect glory is not glory.'

The whole world is incapable of judging either right or wrong. But it is certain that actionless action can judge both right and wrong. Perfect happiness is keeping yourself alive, and only actionless action can have this effect. This is why I want to say:

> Heaven does without doing through its purity,
> Earth does without doing through its calmness.

Thus the two combine their actionless action and all forms of life are changed and thus come out again to live! Wonder of wonders, they have not come from anywhere! All life is mysterious and emerges from actionless action. There is a saying that Heaven and Earth take actionless action, but yet nothing remains undone. Amongst the people, who can follow such actionless action?

[. . .]

Uncle Legless and Uncle Cripple were touring the area of the Hill of the Dark Prince and the zone of Kun Lun where the Yellow Emperor stayed. Without warning a willow tree suddenly shot up out of Uncle Cripple's left elbow. He was certainly most surprised and somewhat put out.

'Sir, do you dislike this?' said Uncle Legless.

'No,' said Uncle Cripple. 'What should I dislike? Life exists through scrounging; if life comes through scrounging, then life is like a dump. Death and birth are like the morning and the night. You and I, Sir, observe the ways of transformation and now I am being transformed. So how could I dislike this?'

Chuang Tzu went to Chu to see an ancient desiccated skull, which he prodded with his riding crop, saying, 'Sir, did you follow some unfortunate course which meant you brought dishonour upon your father and mother and family and so end up like this? Sir, was it perhaps the cold and hunger that reduced you to this? Sir, perhaps it was just the steady succession of springs and autumns that brought you to this?'

So saying, he pulled the skull towards him and lay down to sleep, using the skull as a head-rest. At midnight he saw the skull in a dream and it said, 'Sir, you gabble on like a public speaker. Every word you say, Sir, shows that you are a man caught up with life. We dead have nothing to do with this. Would you like to hear a discourse upon death, Sir?'

'Certainly,' said Chuang Tzu.

The skull told him, 'The dead have no lord over them, no servants below them. There is none of the work associated with the four seasons, so we live as if our springs and autumns were like Heaven and Earth, unending. Make no mistake, a king facing south could not be happier.'

Chuang Tzu could not believe this and said, 'If I got the Harmonizer of Destinies to bring you back to life, Sir, with a body, flesh and blood, and companions, wouldn't you like that?'

The skull frowned, looked aggrieved and said, 'Why should I want to cast away happiness greater than that of kings and become a burdened human being again?'

[. . .]

Confucius said: 'Have you never heard this story before? Once upon a time, a seabird alighted in the capital city of Lu. The Earl of Lu carried it in procession to the ancestral shrine, where he played the Nine Shao music and offered the offerings of the sacrifice to it. However, the poor bird just looked confused and lost and did not eat a single piece of meat, nor did it drink even one cup of wine, and within three days it died. The problem was trying to feed a bird on what you eat rather than what a bird needs.

'To feed a bird so it survives, let it live in the midst of the forest, gambol on the shores and inlets, float on the rivers and lakes, devour mudfish and tiddlers, go with the flock, either flying or resting, and be as it wishes. Birds dislike hearing human voices, never mind all the other noises and trouble! If you try to make them happy by playing the Nine Shao music in the area around their lakes, when the birds hear it they will fly away. If the animals hear it, they will run away and hide and if the fish hear it they will dive down to escape. Only the people, if they hear it, will come together to listen.

'Fish can live in water quite contentedly, but if people try it, they die, for different beings need different contexts which are right and proper for them. This is why the ancient sages never expected just one response from the rest of the creatures nor tried to make them conform. Titles should not be over-stretched in trying to capture reality and ideas should be only applied when appropriate, for this is not only sensible, it will bring good fortune.'

[. . .]

The priest of the ancestors looked into the pigsty and said, 'What's so bad about dying? I fatten you up for three months, then I undergo spiritual discipline for ten days, fast for three days, lay out the white reeds, carve up your shoulders and rump and lay them on the place of sacrifice. Surely you're OK with that, aren't you?'

It is, however, true to say that from the perspective of the pig it would be better to eat oats and bran and stay there in the pigsty. It is also true that, looking at this from my perspective, I'd like to be honoured as an important official while alive and, when I die, be buried with a horse-drawn hearse, lying upon a bed of feathers. I could live with that! From the pig's point of view, I wouldn't give a penny for such a life, but from my point of view, I'd be very content, though I wonder why I perceive things so differently from a pig?

PART II

Grasping the Purpose of Life

If you have grasped the purpose of life there is no point in trying to make life into something it is not or cannot be.

If you have grasped the purpose of destiny, there is no point in trying to change it through knowledge.

If you wish to care for your body, first of all take care of material things, though even when you have all the things you want, the body can still be uncared for.

Since you have life, you must first of all take care that this does not abandon the body. However, it is possible for the body to retain its life, but still not be sustained. Birth cannot be avoided, nor death be prevented. How ridiculous! To see the people of this generation who believe that simply caring for the body will preserve life. But if caring for the body is not sufficient to sustain life, why does the world continue to do this? It may be worthless, but nevertheless it cannot be neglected, we are unable to avoid it.

If someone wishes to stop doing anything to sustain the body, they are advised to leave this world, for by leaving they can be free from any commitments, and, being free from commitments, they can be virtuous and peaceful. Being virtuous and peaceful, they can be born again like others and, being born again, they approach close to the Tao. But why is it such a good idea to leave the troubles of this existence and to forget the purpose of life? If you leave the troubles of existence, your body will not be wearied; if you forget life, your energy will not be damaged. Thus, with your body and energy harmonized, you can become one with Heaven. Heaven and Earth are the father and mother of all life. Together they create a form, apart they create a beginning. If body and energy are without fault, this is known as being able to adapt. Strengthened and again strengthened, you come back again to assist Heaven.

Master Lieh Tzu asked gatekeeper Yin, 'Only the perfect man can walk under water and not drown, can walk on fire without burning, and can pass over the multitude of forms of life without fear. I would like to ask, how does the perfect one do this?'

Gatekeeper Yin replied, 'It is because he preserves his original breath and this has nothing to do with knowledge, work, persistence or bravery. Sit down, and I will tell you all about it.

'Everything has a face, forms, sounds and colour: these are just appearances. How is it possible that this thing and that thing are separated from each other? Indeed, why should any of them be viewed as truly the first of all beings? They are just forms and colours, and nothing more. However, everything arises from what is formless and descends into that which is changeless.

'If you grasp and follow this, using it to the full, nothing can stand in your way! It means being able to reside within limits which have no limit, be secluded within boundaries which have no beginning, ramble to where both the beginning and the end of all life is; combine the essential nature, nourish the original breath, harmonize Virtue and, by following this path, commune with the origin of all life. Someone like this guards his unity with

Heaven, his spirit is without fault, and thus nothing can get inside and attack him!

'If a drunk falls out of his carriage, even if the carriage is going very fast, he will not die. He is just the same as others, bone and joints, but he is not injured, for his spirit is united. Since he does not realize he was travelling, he has no idea that he has fallen out, so neither life nor death, alarm nor fear can affect him, and he just bumps into things without any anxiety or injury.

'If it is possible to stay united through being drunk on wine, just imagine how much more together one could be if united with Heaven! The sage retreats to the serenity of Heaven, as a result nothing causes him harm. Even someone who is out for revenge does not break his opponent's sword. Nor does someone get cross with a tile that just fell on him, no matter how upset he is. Instead, we should recognize that everything under Heaven is united. Thus it is possible to get rid of chaos, violence and warfare and of the rigours of punishment and execution, for this is the Tao.

'Do not hearken to the Heavenly in humanity, but listen to the Heavenly in Heaven, for paying attention to Heaven's Virtue is life-giving, while attending to humanity damages life. Do not cast aside the Heavenly, and do not ignore the human aspect: then the people will draw closer to the realization of Truth!'

[. . .]

Confucius was sightseeing in Lu Liang, where the waterfall is thirty fathoms high and the river races along for forty miles, so fast that neither fish nor any other creature can swim in it. He saw one person dive in and he assumed that this person wanted to embrace death, perhaps because of some anxiety, so he placed his followers along the bank and they prepared to pull him out. However, the swimmer, having gone a hundred yards, came out, and walked nonchalantly along the bank, singing a song with water dripping off him.

Confucius pursued him and said, 'I thought you were a ghost, but now I see, Sir, that you are a man. I wish to enquire, do you have a Tao for swimming under the water?'

He said, 'No, I have no Tao. I started with what I knew, matured my innate nature and allow destiny to do the rest. I go in with the currents and come out with the flow, just going with the Tao of the water and never being concerned. That is how I survive.'

Confucius said, 'What do you mean when you say you started with what you knew, matured your innate nature and allow destiny to do the rest?'

He said, 'I was born on the dry land and feel content on the land, where I know what I know. I was nurtured by the water, and felt safe there: that reflects my innate nature. I am not sure why I do this, but I am certain that this is destiny.'

Woodcarver Ching carved a piece of wood to form a bell support, and those who saw it were astonished because it looked as if ghosts or spirits had done it. The Marquis of Lu saw it, and asked, 'Where does your art come from?'

'I am just a woodcarver,' Ching replied. 'How could I have "art"? One thing is certain, though, that when I carve a bell support, I do not allow it to exhaust my original breath, so I take care to calm my heart. After I have fasted for three days, I give no thought to praise, reward, titles or income. After I have fasted for five days, I give no thought to glory or blame, to skill or stupidity. After I have fasted for seven days, I am so still that I forget whether I have four limbs and a body. By then the Duke and his court have ceased to exist as far as I am concerned. All my energy is focused and external concerns have gone. After that I depart and enter the mountain forest, and explore the Heavenly innate nature of the trees; once I find one with a perfect shape, I can see for certain the possibility of a bell support and I set my hand to the task; if I cannot see the possibility, I leave it be. By so doing, I harmonize the Heavenly with Heaven, and perhaps this is why it is thought that my carvings are done by spirits!'

[. . .]

Workman Chui could draw as straight as a T-square or as curved as a compass, because his fingers could follow the changes and his heart did not obstruct. Thus his mind was one and never blocked. The feet can be forgotten when you walk in comfortable shoes. The waist can be forgotten when your belt fits comfortably. Knowledge can forget yes and no, if the heart journeys contentedly. Nothing changes inside, nothing proceeds from outside, if you respond to what occurs in a contented way. By starting with what is contented, not undergoing that which is disturbing, it is possible to know the contentment of forgetting what contentment is.

[. . .]

Chuang Tzu was walking through the heart of the mountains when he saw a huge verdant tree. A wood-cutter stopped beside the tree, but did not cut it. When asked why he didn't he said, 'It's no good.' Chuang Tzu said, 'Because this tree is not considered useful, it can follow all the years Heaven has given it.'

The Master came out of the mountains and stayed a night at a friend's house. This man was delighted and told his son to kill a goose and cook it. The son answered, saying, 'One goose can cackle, the other one can't. Tell me which one to prepare?' The father replied, 'Prepare the one that does not cackle.'

On the next day Chuang Tzu's followers asked him, 'Yesterday there was a tree in the heart of the mountains which was able to live all the years Heaven gives because it is no use. Now, at your friend's house, there is a goose who dies because it is no use. Teacher, what do you think of this?'

Chuang Tzu laughed and said, 'Personally, I'd find a position between useful and useless. This position between useful and useless might seem a good position, but I tell you it is not, for trouble will pursue you. It would certainly not be so, however, if you were to mount upon the Virtue of the Tao;

'never certain, never directed,
never praised, never condemned,
on the one hand a dragon, on the other a snake,
going as it seems appropriate.
Now up, now down,
using harmony as your guide,
floating on the source of all life.

'Let things be, but don't allow things to treat you as just an object, then you cannot be led into difficulties! This is the path taken by Shen Nung and the Yellow Emperor. Now, however, because of the multitudinous varieties of species and the ethical codes of humanity, things certainly aren't what they were!

> 'There is unity only in order to divide;
> fulfilment only in order to collapse;
> a cutting edge is blunted;
> those who are elevated are overthrown;
> ambition is thwarted;
> the wise are conspired against;
> the fools are conned.

'So what can be trusted? My followers, just the Tao and its Virtue!'

[. . .]

Confucius was besieged in the area between Chen and Tsai and had no hot food for seven days. The Grand Duke Jen came out to express his concern and said, 'Master, do you think you will die?'

'Certainly,' said Confucius.

'Master, are you frightened by death?'

'Certainly.'

'I would like to tell you the Tao of never dying,' said Jen. 'There is a bird that dwells in the Eastern Ocean called Helpless. This bird is helpless for it flips and flops, flips and flops, as if it had no strength, flying only with the assistance of the other birds and jostling to return to the nest. None of them likes to be in front or behind, preferring to pick away at what others leave. Thus, when the bird flies, it is never alone, and no others outside the flock, such as humans, can do it any harm, so it avoids disasters.

'The straight tree is the first to be chopped down; the well of sweet water is the first to run dry. Sir, your intention is to display your knowledge in order to astonish the ignorant, and by developing your self, to cast a light upon the crudeness of others. You shine, you positively glow, as if you carried with you the sun and moon. All this is why you cannot avoid disasters.

'I have heard the great fulfilment man say, "The boastful have done nothing worthwhile, those who do something worthwhile will see it fade, fame soon disappears." There are few who can forget success and fame and just return to being ordinary citizens again! The Tao moves all, but the perfect man does not stand in its light, his Virtue moves all, but he does not seek fame. He is empty and plain, and seems crazy. Anonymous, abdicating power, he has no interest in work or fame. So he doesn't criticize others and they don't criticize him. The perfect man is never heard, so why, Sir, do you so want to be?'

Confucius said, 'Splendid!' then said farewell to his friends, left his followers and retired into a great marsh, put on animal skins and rough cloth and lived off acorns and chestnuts. He went out amongst the animals and they were not afraid, amongst the birds and they did not fly away. If the birds and animals were not alarmed, then neither should people be either!

Confucius asked Master Sang Hu, 'I have been exiled

from Lu twice, a tree was toppled on top of me in Sung, all records of me have been wiped out in Wei, I was impoverished in Shang and besieged in Chen and Tsai. I have had to endure so many troubles. My friends and acquaintances have wandered off and my followers have begun deserting me. But why is this happening?'

Master Sang Hu said, 'Have you not heard of the man of Chia who ran away? Lin Hui threw aside his jade emblem worth a thousand pieces of gold, tied his son to his back and hurried away. People asked, "Was it because the boy was worth more? Surely a child isn't that valuable. Was it because of all the effort required to carry the jade? But surely a child is even more trouble. So why throw away the jade emblem worth a thousand pieces of gold and rush off with the young child on your back?" Lin Hui told them, "It was greed that brought me and the jade emblem together, but it was Heaven that linked my son and me together."

'When the ties between people are based upon profit, then when troubles come, people part easily. When people are brought together by Heaven, then when troubles come, they hold together. To hold together or to separate, these are two very different things. The relationship with a nobleman can be as bland as water, that with a mean-spirited person sickly sweet as wine. However, the blandness of the nobleman can develop into affection, but the sweetness of the mean-spirited person develops into revulsion. That which unites for no apparent reason, will fall apart for no apparent reason.'

[. . .]

Chuang Tzu, dressed in a worn, patched gown made of coarse cloth and with shoes held together with string, went to visit the King of Wei. The King of Wei said, 'Why are you in such a state, Master?'

Chuang Tzu replied, 'This is poverty but not distress. If a scholar has the Tao and the Virtue but is unable to use them, that is distress. If his clothes are worn and shoes held together with string, that is poverty but not distress. This is known as not being around at the right time. Your Majesty, have you never seen monkeys climbing? When they are amongst plane trees, the oaks and camphor trees, they cling to branches and leaves with such ease that not even the archers Yi or Peng Meng could spot them. However, when they are amongst the prickly mulberry, thorny date trees and other spiky bushes, they move cautiously, looking from side to side, shaking with fear. This is not because their sinews and bones have gone stiff or unable to bend, but because the monkeys are not in their own environment and so cannot use their skills. Now that I find myself living with a benighted leader and with rebellious ministers above me, how can I avoid distress?

[. . .]

Chuang Tzu was wandering through the park at Tiao Ling, when he saw a strange jackdaw come flying from the south. Its wing-span measured seven feet and its eyes were large, about an inch across. It brushed against Chuang Tzu's forehead as it passed and then came to rest in a copse of chestnut trees. Chuang Tzu said, 'What sort of bird is this, with wings so vast but going nowhere, eyes so large but it can't see properly?' Hitching up his robe, he hurried after it with his crossbow in order to take a pot shot at it. On the way he saw a cicada which was basking in a beautiful shady spot, without a thought for its bodily safety. Suddenly, a praying mantis stretched forth its feelers and prepared to spring upon the cicada, so engrossed in the hunt that it forgot its own safety. The strange jackdaw swept down and seized them both, likewise forgetting its own safety in the excitement of the prize. Chuang Tzu sighed with compassion and said, 'Ah! So it is that one thing brings disaster upon another, and then upon itself!' He cast aside his crossbow and was on his way out, when the forester chased after him, shouting at him for being a poacher.

Chuang Tzu went home and was depressed for three months. Lin Chou, who was with him, asked him, 'Master, why are you so miserable?'

Chuang Tzu said, 'I was so concerned with my body that I forgot my self. It was like looking into cloudy water, thinking it was really clear. Furthermore, I heard my Master say once, "When associating with the locals, act like a local." So I went out walking in the park at Tiao Ling and forgot my own self. A strange jackdaw touched my forehead, then settled in a copse of chestnut trees and there forgot its own true being. The forester thought I was to blame. This is why I'm miserable.'

[. . .]

Confucius went to see Lao Tzu and found him washing his hair. He had spread it out over his shoulders to dry. He stood there without moving, as if no one else existed in the world. Confucius stood quietly and then, after a while, quietly came into his vision and said, 'Were my eyes dazzled, is this really you? Just now, Sir, your body was as still as an old dead tree. You seemed to have no thought in your head, as if you were in another world and standing utterly alone.'

'I let my heart ponder upon the origin of beginnings,' said Lao Tzu.

'What do you mean?' asked Confucius.

'The heart may try to reason this out but doesn't understand it, and the mouth may hang open but can't find words to say. Still, I will attempt to describe this to you. Perfect yin is harsh and cold, perfect yang is awesome and fiery. Harshness and coldness emanate from Earth, awesomeness and fieriness emanate from Heaven. The two mingle and join, and from their conjunction comes to birth everything that lives. Maybe there is one who controls and ensures all this, but if so, then no one has seen any form or shape. Decay and growth, fullness and emptiness, at one time dark, at another bright, the changes of the sun and the transformation of the moon, these go by day after day, but no one has seen what causes this. Life has its origin from which it emerges and death has its place to which it returns. Beginning and end follow each other inexorably and no one knows of any end to this. If this is not so, then who is the origin and guide?'

'I want to ask what it means to wander like this,' said Confucius.

Lao Tzu said, 'To obtain this is perfect beauty and perfect happiness, and to obtain perfect beauty and wander in perfect happiness is to be a perfect man.'

'I would like to hear how this is done,' said Confucius.

Lao Tzu replied, 'Creatures that eat grass are not put

out by a change of pasture. Creatures that are born in the water are not put out by a change of water. They can live with a minor change, but not with a change to that which is the most significant. Joy, anger, sadness and happiness do not enter into their breasts. All under Heaven, all forms of life, come together in the One. Obtain the One and merge with it and all your four limbs and hundred joints will become just dust and ashes. For death and birth, ending and beginning are nothing more than the sequence of day and night. Then you will never be disturbed in your contentment by such trifles as gain and loss, for example, good fortune or bad! Those who ignore the status of authority, casting it aside like so much mud, they know that their own self is of greater significance than any title. The value of your self lies within and is not affected by what happens externally. The constant transformation of all forms of life is like a beginning without end. What is there in this to disturb your heart? Those who comprehend the Tao are freed from all this.'

'Master,' said Confucius, 'your Virtue is like that of Heaven and Earth, but even you have to resort to these perfect words to guide you. Who amongst the great men of antiquity could have lived this out?'

Lao Tzu replied, 'I certainly do not. The flowing of the stream does nothing, but it follows its nature. The perfect man does the same with regard to Virtue. He does nothing to cultivate it, but all is affected by its presence. He is like the height of Heaven: natural; or the solidity of Earth, the brightness of sun and moon: all natural. There is no need to cultivate this!'

[. . .]

Chuang Tzu went to see Duke Ai of Lu. Duke Ai said, 'There are many learned scholars in Lu but few of them study your works, Master.'

Chuang Tzu said, 'Lu has few learned ones.'

Duke Ai said, 'There are men wearing the dress of learned scholars throughout the state of Lu. How can you say there are few?'

Chuang Tzu said, 'I have heard that those learned ones who wear round caps on their heads, know the seasons of Heaven; those who wear square shoes know the shape of the Earth; those who tie semi-circular disks to their belts deal perfectly with all that comes before them. But a nobleman can follow the Tao without having to dress the part. Indeed, he might wear the dress but not understand the Tao at all! Should my Lord not be sure on this point, why not issue an order of state saying, "Any wearing the dress but not practising the Tao will be executed!"'

This is exactly what Duke Ai did, and five days later throughout the kingdom of Lu not a single learned one wore the dress! Only one old man wore the dress of the learned and stood at the Duke's gate. The Duke immediately called him in and discussed the affairs of the kingdom with him, and though they went through a thousand issues and tens of thousands of digressions, the old man was never at a loss.

Chuang Tzu said, 'So, in the whole kingdom of Lu there is just this one man who is among the learned ones. How can you claim there are many?'

PART 12

Do Not Ask about the Tao

Knowledge strolled north to the shores of the Dark Waters, scaled the mount of Secret Heights and came upon Words-of-Actionless-Action. Knowledge said to Words-of-Actionless-Action, 'I want to ask you something. What sort of thought and reflection does it take to know the Tao? In what sort of place and in what sorts of ways should we undertake to rest in the Tao? What sort of path and what sort of plans do we need to obtain the Tao?' These three questions he asked of Words-of-Actionless-Action, but he did not answer. Not only did he not answer, he had no idea what to answer.

Knowledge did not obtain any answers, so he travelled to the White Waters of the south, climbed up on to the top of Doubt Curtailed and there caught sight of Wild-and-Surly. Knowledge put the same question to Wild-and-Surly. Wild-and-Surly said, 'Ah ha! I know, and I will tell you.' In the middle of saying this, he forgot what he was going to say!

Knowledge did not obtain any answers, so he went back to the Emperor's palace to see the Yellow Emperor and to ask him. The Yellow Emperor said, 'Practise having no thoughts and no reflections and you will come to know the Tao. Only when you have no place and can see no way forward will you find rest in the Tao. Have no path and no plans and you will obtain the Tao.'

Knowledge said to the Yellow Emperor, 'You and I

know this, but the others did not know, so which of us is actually right?'

The Yellow Emperor said, 'Words-of-Actionless-Action was truly right. Wild-and-Surly seems right. In the end, you and I are not close to it.

> 'Those who understand, do not say.
> Those who say, do not understand.
> And so the sage follows the teachings without words.
> The Tao cannot be made to occur,
> Virtue cannot be sought after.
> However, benevolence can be undertaken,
> righteousness can be striven for,
> rituals can be adhered to.
> It is said, "When the Tao was lost, Virtue appeared;
> when Virtue was lost, benevolence appeared;
> when benevolence was lost, righteousness appeared;
> when righteousness was lost, ritual appeared.
> Rituals are just the frills on the hem of the Tao,
> and are signs of impending disorder."

'It is said, "One who follows the Tao daily does less and less. As he does less and less, he eventually arrives at actionless action. Having achieved actionless action, there is nothing which is not done." Now that we have become active, if we wish to return to our original state, we will find it very difficult! Who but the great man could change this?

> 'Life follows death and death is the forerunner of life.
> Who can know their ways?

Human life begins with the original breath;
When it comes together there is life,
When it is dispersed, there is death.'

[. . .]

Confucius said to Lao Tzu, 'Now, today, you seem relaxed, so I would like to ask about the perfect Tao.'

Lao Tzu said, 'You should cleanse and purify your heart through fasting and austerities, wash your spirit to make it clean and repress your knowledge. The Tao is profound and almost impossible to describe! I will attempt to offer some understanding of it:

'The brightly shining is born from the deeply dark;
that which is orderly is born from the formless;
the spiritual is born from the Tao;
the roots of the body are born from the seminal
    essence;
all forms of life give each other shape through birth.
Those with nine apertures are born from the womb,
while those with eight are born from eggs.
Of its coming there is no trace,
no sign of its departure,
neither entering the gate nor dwelling anywhere,
open to all the four directions.
Those who travel with the Tao will be strong in
    body,
sincere and profound in their thought,
clear of sight and hearing,
using their hearts without tiring,
responding to all without prejudice.
As a result of this, Heaven is high and Earth wide,

the sun and moon move and everything flourishes.
This is the Tao!

'Even the broadest knowledge does not comprehend it.
Reason does not mean wisdom, so the sage casts
    these aside.
There is something which is complete, no matter
    what you add;
is not diminished, no matter what you take away.
This is what the sage holds to.
It is as the ocean, deeply deep,
as the mountains, high and proud,
its end is its beginning,
it carries all forms of life and never fails.
The Tao of the nobleman is just external garb!
That which sustains all forms of life and never falters,
    this is the true Tao!'
[. . .]

Great Purity asked Endless, 'Sir, do you know the Tao?'

'I do not know it,' said Endless.

Then he asked Actionless Action, who replied, 'I know the Tao.'

'Sir,' asked Great Purity, 'about your knowledge of the Tao, do you have some special hints?'

'I have.'

'What are they?'

Actionless Action said, 'I know that the Tao can elevate and bring low, bind together and separate. These are the hints I would give you to know the Tao.'

With these different answers Great Purity went to No

Beginning and said, 'Between Endless's statement that he doesn't know, and Actionless Action's statement that he does know, I am left wondering which of these is right and which is wrong.'

No Beginning said, 'Not to know is profound and to know is shallow. To be without knowledge is to be inward, to know is to be outward.'

Then indeed did Great Purity cast his eyes upward and sigh, 'Not to know is to know and to know is not to know! Who knows about not knowing about knowing?'

No Beginning said:

> 'The Tao cannot be heard: what is heard is not
>   the Tao.
> The Tao cannot be seen: what can be seen is
>   not the Tao.
> The Tao cannot be spoken: what is spoken is not
>   the Tao.
> Do we know what form gives form to the formless?
> The Tao has no name.'

No Beginning continued:

'To be questioned about the Tao and to give an answer means that you don't know the Tao.

'One who asks about the Tao has never understood anything about the Tao.

'Do not ask about the Tao, for the asking is not appropriate, nor can the question be answered, because it is like asking those in dire extremity. To answer what cannot be answered is to show no inner understanding. When someone without inner understanding waits for an answer from those in dire extremity, they illustrate that they neither grasp where they stand outwardly nor understand the great Beginning within. So they cannot cross the Kun Lun mountains nor wander in the great Void.'

[. . .]

Nan Jung Chu gathered his provisions and set off, and after seven days and seven nights he arrived at the home of Lao Tzu.

'Have you come from Chu?' said Lao Tzu, and Nan Jung Chu replied, 'I have.'

'So, Sir, why have you brought this great crowd of other people with you?' Nan Jung Chu spun round and looked behind him in astonishment.

'Sir, don't you understand what I am saying?' said Lao Tzu.

Nan Jung Chu hung his head in shame and then looked up, sighed and said, 'Now I can't remember what to say in response and have therefore also forgotten what I was going to ask.'

'What are you saying?' said Lao Tzu.

'Do I have any understanding?' said Nan Jung Chu. 'People will call me a fool. Do I understand? This just upsets me. If I am not benevolent, then I distress others. If I am benevolent, then I distress myself. If I am not righteous, then I harm others. If I am righteous, then I upset myself. How can I get out of all this? These three issues perplex me, so following Chu's instructions I have come to ask you about them.'

Lao Tzu replied, 'Just now I looked deep into your eyes and I could see what sort of a person you are. What you have just said convinces me I am right. You are bewildered and confused, as if you had lost your father and mother and were looking for them using a pole to reach the bottom of the sea. You are lost and frightened. You want to rediscover your self and your innate nature but you haven't a clue how to set about this. What a sorry state you are in!'

Nan Jung Chu asked to be allowed to go into his room. He sought to develop the good and rid himself of the bad. After ten days of misery he came out and went to see Lao Tzu again.

'I can see that you have been washing and purifying yourself thoroughly,' said Lao Tzu, 'but you are still impure despite the outward cleanliness. Something is stirring inside you and there is still something rotten within. Outside influences will press upon you and you will find it impossible to control them. It is wiser to shut the gate of your inner self against them. Likewise, when interior influences disturb you and you find it impossible to control them, then shut the gate of your self so as to keep them in. To struggle against both the outside and inside influences is more than even one who follows the Tao and its Virtue can control, so how much more difficult it is for one who is just starting out along the Tao.'

Nan Jung Chu said, 'A villager fell ill and his neighbour asked how he was. He was able to describe his illness, even though he had never suffered from it before. When I ask you about the great Tao, it is like drinking medicine that makes me feel worse than before. I would like to know about the normal method for protecting one's life, that is all.'

'The basic way of protecting life – can you embrace the One?' said Lao Tzu. 'Can you hold it fast? Can you tell good from bad fortune without using the divination of the tortoise shell or the yarrow sticks? Do you know when to stop? Do you know when to desist? Can you forget others and concentrate upon your inner self? Can you escape lures? Can you be sincere? Can you be a little baby? The baby cries all day long but its throat never becomes hoarse: that indeed is perfect harmony. The baby clenches its fists all day long but never gets cramp, it holds fast to Virtue. The baby stares all day long but it is not affected by what is outside it. It moves without knowing where, it sits without knowing where it is sitting, it is quietly placid and rides the flow of events. This is how to protect life.'

'So this is what it takes to be a perfect man?' said Nan Jung Chu.

'Indeed no. This is what is known as the melting of the ice, the dissolving of the cold. Are you up to it? The perfect man is as one with others in seeking his food from the Earth and his joy from Heaven. However, he remains detached from consideration of profit and gain from others, does not get embroiled in plots and schemes nor in grandiose projects. Alert and unceasing he goes, simple and unpretentious he comes. This indeed is called the way to protect life.'

'So it is this which is his perfection?'

'Not quite,' replied Lao Tzu. 'Just now I asked you, "Can you become a little baby?" The baby acts without knowing why and moves without knowing where. Its body is like a rotting branch and its heart is like cold ashes. Being like this, neither bad fortune will affect it nor good fortune draw near. Having neither bad fortune nor good, it is not affected by the misfortune that comes to most others!'

[. . .]

There is a saying:

> 'Perfect behaviour does not discriminate
> amongst people;
> perfect righteousness takes no account of things;
> perfect knowledge makes no plans;
> perfect benevolence exhibits no emotion;
> perfect faith makes no oath of sincerity.'

> Suppress the whims of the will and untie the
> mistakes of the heart.
> Expunge the knots of Virtue,
> unblock the flow of the Tao.

> Honours and wealth,
> distinctions and authority,
> fame and gain,
> these six are formed by the illusions of the will.

> Looks and style,
> beauty and reason,
> thrill of life and memories,
> these six are the faults of the heart.

> Hatred and desire,
> joy and anger,

sadness and happiness,
these six are the knots of Virtue.

Rejection and acceptance,
giving and taking,
knowledge and ability,
these six are the impediments to the free flow
 of the Tao.

When these four sets of six no longer trouble
 the breast,
then you will be centred.
Being centred, you will be calm.
Being calm, you will be enlightened.
Being enlightened, you will be empty.
Being empty, you will be in actionless action,
But with actionless action nothing remains undone.
The Tao is the centrepiece of the devotions of Virtue.
Life is the brightness of Virtue.
Innate nature is what motivates life.
[. . .]

Chuang Tzu's family were poor so he went to borrow
some rice from the Marquis of Chien Ho. The Marquis
of Chien Ho said, 'Of course. I am about to receive the
tax from the people and will give you three hundred
pieces of gold – is that enough?'

Chuang Tzu flushed with anger and said, 'On my way
here yesterday I heard a voice calling me. I looked around
and saw a large fish in the carriage rut. I said, "Fish! What
are you doing there?" He said, "I am Minister of the
Waves in the Eastern Ocean. Sire, do you have a measure

of water you could give me?" Well, I told him, "I am
going south to visit the Kings of Wu and Yueh and after
that I would redirect the course of the Western River so
it will flow up to you. Would that do?" The large fish
flushed with anger and said, "I am out of my very element, I have nowhere to go. Give me just a little water and
I can survive. But giving me such an answer as that means
you will only ever find me again on a dried fish stall!" '

[. . .]

> The great One knows,
> the great mystery reveals,
> the great yin observes,
> the great eye sees,
> the great equal is the origin,
> the great skill creates it,
> the great trust touches it,
> the great judge holds fast to it.

Heaven is in everything: follow the light, hide in the
cloudiness and begin in what is. Do this and your understanding will be like not understanding and your wisdom
will be like not being wise. By not being wise you will
become wise later. When you ask questions, set no limits,
even though they cannot be limitless. Although things
seem to be sometimes going up and sometimes descending, sometimes slipping away, nevertheless there is a reality, the same today as in the past. It does not change, for
nothing can affect it. Could we not say it is one great harmony? So why shouldn't we ask about it and why are you
so confused? If we use that which does not confuse to
understand that which does confuse, then we can come

back to that which does not confuse. This will be the great unconfusing.

[. . .]

'The four seasons each have their own original life,
and Heaven does not discriminate,
so the cycle is fulfilled.
The five government offices have different roles,
but the ruler does not discriminate,
so the state is well run.
The great man does not discriminate
between war and peace,
so his Virtue is perfect.
All the forms of life are different,
but the Tao does not discriminate,
so it has no name.
Being nameless, it is also actionless action,
yet all life occurs.
The seasons end and begin;
the generations change and transform.
Inauspicious and auspicious fortune falls upon you,
sometimes unwelcomed,
other times welcomed.
Settle into your own views,
argue with others,
at times condemn those who are upright,
then those who are bent.
You should be like a great marsh land
with space for a hundred kinds of trees.
Or be like a great mountain
where the trees and grasses rest on the same ground.
This is what is meant by Talk of the Villages.'

PART 13

Can I Ask You about Truth?

In the past King Wen of Chao loved swords. Specialists came to his gate, over three thousand of them, all experts in swordsmanship. They were his guests. Day and night they fought before him until the dead or wounded each year were more than a hundred. But the King never ceased to be delighted at watching them. This went on for three years, then the country began to fall apart and the other princes began to plot its overthrow.

Crown Prince Kuei was distressed by this, and he presented the situation to his followers:

'If there is anyone here who can persuade the King to put away these swordsmen, I will give him a thousand pieces of gold,' he said. His followers replied,

'Chuang Tzu can do this.'

The Crown Prince sent an ambassador with a thousand pieces of gold to Chuang Tzu. Chuang Tzu refused the gold but returned with the ambassador. He came in to see the Crown Prince and said, 'Oh Prince, what is it you wish to tell me that you send me a thousand pieces of gold?'

'I have heard, Sir, that you are an illustrious sage,' said the Crown Prince. 'The gift of a thousand pieces of gold was a gift for your attendants. However, you have refused to accept this, so what more dare I say?'

Chuang Tzu said, 'I have heard that the Crown Prince

wants to use me to help the King give up his abiding passion. If in trying to do so I upset the King and fail to achieve what you hope for, then I might be executed. So what use would the gold be to me then? Or, if I could get the King to give up, and fulfil your hopes, what is there in this whole kingdom of Chao that I could not ask for and be given?'

'You're right,' said the Crown Prince. 'However the King will only see swordsmen.'

'That's all right. I'm quite good with a sword,' replied Chuang Tzu.

'Fair enough,' said the Crown Prince, 'but the swordsmen the King sees are all tousle-headed with spiky beards, wearing loose caps held on with simple, rough straps and robes that are cut short behind. They look about them fiercely and talk only of their sport. The King loves all this. Now, if you go in wearing your scholar's garb you will start off on completely the wrong foot.'

'With your permission I will get a full swordsman's outfit,' said Chuang Tzu.

Within three days he had got this and returned to see the Crown Prince. The Crown Prince took him to see the King, who drew his sword and sat waiting for him. Chuang Tzu walked slowly into the hall through the main door. When he saw the King, he did not bow.

'What instruction have you for me, that you have persuaded the Crown Prince about beforehand?' demanded the King.

'I have heard that the King likes swords and so I have brought my sword for the King to see.'

'What use is your sword in combat?'

'My sword can kill one person every ten paces, and after a thousand miles it is not faltering.'

The King was pleased and said, 'There can be no one else like you under Heaven!'

'A fine swordsman opens with a feint then gives ground, following up with a cut, stalling his opponent before he can react,' replied Chuang Tzu. 'I would like to show you my skills.'

'Rest awhile in your rooms, Master, and await my commands,' said the King. 'I shall make arrangements for the contest and I will call you.'

The King spent the next seven days testing his swordsmen. More than sixty died or were severely wounded, leaving five or six who were selected and commanded to present themselves in the hall. Then he called in Chuang Tzu and said, 'Now, this very day I shall pit you against these men to show your skills.'

'I have longed for such an opportunity,' said Chuang Tzu.

'Sir, what sort of sword will you choose, long or short?' asked the King.

'Any kind will do,' said Chuang Tzu, 'but I have three swords, any of which I could use if the King agrees. But first I would like to say something about them and then use them.'

'I would like to hear about these three swords,' said the King.

'I have the sword of the Son of Heaven, the sword of the noble Prince and the sword of the commoner,' said Chuang Tzu.

'What is this sword of the Son of Heaven?'

'The Son of Heaven's sword has as its point the Valley of Yen, and the Great Wall and Chi and Tai mountains as its blade edge. Chin and Wey are its ridge, Chou and Sung are its hilt and Han and Wei its sheath. On all four sides it is surrounded by barbarians and it is wrapped in the four seasons. The Sea of Po encompasses it and the eternal mountains of Chang are its belt. The five elements control it and it enacts what punishment and compassion dictate. It comes out in obedience to yin and yang, stands alert in spring and summer and goes into action in autumn and winter. Thrust forward, there is nothing in front of it; lift it high, and there is nothing above it; swing it low, and there is nothing below it; spin it around, there is nothing encompassing it. Raised high, it cleaves the firmaments; swung low, it severs the very veins of the Earth. Use this sword but once and all the rulers revert to obedience; all below Heaven submit. This is the sword of the Son of Heaven.'

King Wen was astonished and seemed to have forgotten everything else.

'What of the sword of the noble Prince?' he asked.

Chuang Tzu said, 'The sword of the noble Prince, its point is sagacious and courageous people; its blade is those of integrity and sincerity; its ridge is those of worth and goodness; its hilt is those who are trustworthy and wise; its sheath is of the brave and outstanding. When this sword is thrust forward, it encounters nothing; when wielded high, it has nothing above it; when swung low, it has nothing below it; when swirled about, it finds nothing near it. Above, its guidance comes from Heaven and it proceeds with the three great lights. Below, it is inspired by the square, stable nature of the earth, proceeding with the flow of the four seasons. In the middle lands it restores harmony to the people and is in balance with the four directions. Use this sword but once and it is like hearing the crash of thunder. Within the four borders everyone obeys the laws and everyone attends to the orders of the ruler. This is the sword of the noble Prince.'

'What of the sword of the commoner?'

'The sword of the commoner is used by those who are tousle-haired with spiky beards, wearing loose caps held on by ordinary coarse cords, with their robes cut short behind. They stare about them fiercely and will only talk about their swordsmanship while fighting before the King. Raised high, it cuts through the neck; swung low, it slices into the liver and lungs. The people who use the sword of the commoner are no better than fighting cocks who at any time can have their lives curtailed. They are useless to the state. Now you, O King, have the position of the Son of Heaven but you make yourself unworthy by associating with the sword of the commoner. This is what I dare to say.'

The King brought him up into his hall where the butler presented a tray of food, while the King strode three times round the room.

'Sire, sit down and calm yourself,' said Chuang Tzu. 'Whatever there was to say about swords has been said.'

Following this, King Wen did not go out for three months and all his swordsmen killed themselves in their own rooms.

[. . .]

Confucius wandered through the Black Curtain Forest and sat down beside the Apricot Tree Altar. His followers started reading their books while Confucius played his lute and sang. He was not even halfway through the song when a fisherman stepped out of his boat and came towards him. His beard and eyebrows were white and his hair was wild, while his sleeves hung down beside him. He walked up the slopes until he reached the drier ground and then stopped, resting his left hand on his knee and his chin in his right hand, and listened until the song was over. Then he called over Tzu Kung and Tzu Lu and the two of them went to him.

'Who is that?' he said, pointing at Confucius.

'He is a nobleman from Lu,' replied Tzu Lu.

The fisherman then enquired as to Confucius' family. Tzu Lu replied, 'The family of Kung.'

'What does this man of Kung do for a living?'

Tzu Lu was working out what to say when Tzu Kung replied, saying, 'This man of the Kung family in his innate nature holds fast to loyalty and faithfulness; in his behaviour he shows benevolence and righteousness; he makes the rituals and music beautiful, and balances human relationships. He pays respect above him to the ruler of his generation and in his dealings with those below him he tries to transform the ordinary people, as he wants to bless the whole world. This is what this man of the Kung family does.'

The fisherman enquired further, 'Does he have any land over which he rules?'

'No,' said Tzu Kung.

'Is he an adviser to a king?'

'No.'

The stranger laughed and backed away, saying, 'So benevolence is benevolence, yet he won't escape without harm to himself. Exhausting the heart and wearing out the body puts his true nature in jeopardy. Sadly, I believe he is far removed from the Tao.'

Tzu Kung went up and told Confucius about this. Confucius laid aside his flute and stood up, saying, 'Maybe he is a sage!' and he went down the slope to find him. He reached the water's edge as the fisherman was about to pole away. Seeing Confucius, he poled back again and confronted him. Confucius stepped back somewhat hastily, bowed twice and went forward.

'What do you want, Sir?' said the stranger.

'Just now, Master, you said a few words but didn't finish,' said Confucius. 'Being unworthy, I do not understand them. So I would like to be with you and to hear even just the sounds of your words in the hope that they might enlighten me!'

'Oh-ho, you have a good love of study, Sir!'

Confucius bowed twice and stood up. 'Ever since I was little I have pursued study, and now here I am sixty-nine years old, yet I have never heard the perfect teaching, so what can I do but keep my heart open?'

The stranger said, 'Like seeks like and each note responds to its own. This is the boundary established by Heaven. I will not discuss that which concerns me, but will concentrate on what you need to know about. You, Sir, are wrapped up in the affairs of the people. The Son of Heaven, the noble princes, the great ministers and the common folk, when these four groups do what is right, there is the beauty of unity. If these four groups break apart, then there is terrible great disorder. If ministers do what they should and the ordinary people are concerned with what they do, then no one infringes upon another.

'Fields in ruin, leaking roofs, lack of food and clothing, unjust taxes, disputes between wives and concubines, disorder between the young and the old, these are what trouble the common folk.

'Inability to do the job, being bored by their work, bad behaviour, carelessness and laziness in those below, failure to succeed, insecurity in employment, these are what trouble the great ministers.

'Lack of loyal ministers, civil war in the kingdom, workmen with no skills, tributes that are worthless, poor positioning at the spring and autumn gatherings, the disquiet of the ruler, these are what trouble the noble princes.

'Yin and yang out of harmony, fluctuations in heat and cold which damage all, oppression and rebellion by nobles, all leading to uprisings, ravage and abuse of the people, the rituals badly performed, the treasury empty, social relationships in turmoil and the people debauched, these are what trouble the Son of Heaven and his people.

'Now, Sir, at the higher end of the scale, you are not a ruler, nor a noble nor even a minister in a court, while at the other end you are not in the office of a great minister with all his portfolios. Nevertheless, you have decided to bring beauty to the rituals and the music and to balance human relationships and thus to reform the ordinary people. Isn't this rather overdoing it?

'Furthermore, there are eight defects that people are

liable to, as well as four evils that affect their affairs, which must not be ignored:

'To be involved with affairs that are not yours is to be overbearing.

'To draw attention to yourself when no one wants you is to be intrusive.

'To suck up to someone with speeches designed to please is to be sycophantic.

'Not to distinguish between good and evil in what others say is to be a flatterer.

'To gossip about other's failings is to be slanderous.

'To separate friends and families is to be malevolent.

'To give false praise in order to hurt others is to be wicked.

'Having no concern for right or wrong, but to be two-faced in order to find out what others know, is to be treacherous.

'These eight defects cause disorder to others and harm to the perpetrator. A nobleman will not befriend one who has them, nor will an enlightened ruler appoint such a person to be a minister.

'With regard to the four evils of which I spoke, they are:

'Ambition – To be fond of taking on vast enterprises, altering and changing the old traditions, thus hoping that you can increase your fame and standing.

'Greediness – To be a know-all and to try and get everything done your way, seizing what others do and claiming it as your own.

'Obstinacy – To see your errors without doing anything to change them and to persist in doing things the wrong way.

'Bigotry – To smile upon someone who agrees with you but when that person disagrees, to disown and despise them.

'These are the four evils. If you can cast aside the eight defects and avoid the four evils, then you are at a point where it is possible to be taught.'

Confucius looked sad and sighed, bowed twice, stood up and said, 'Lu has exiled me twice, I have fled from Wei, they have felled a tree on me in Sung and laid siege to me between Chen and Tsai. I have no idea what I did to be so misunderstood. Why was I subject to these four forms of trouble?'

The stranger looked distressed, then his expression changed and he said, 'It is very difficult, Sir, to make you understand! There was once a man who was frightened by his own shadow and scared of his own footprints, so he tried to escape them by running away. But every time he lifted his foot and brought it down, he made more footprints, and no matter how fast he ran, his shadow never left him. Thinking he was running too slowly, he ran faster, never ceasing until finally he exhausted himself and collapsed and died. He had no idea that by simply sitting in the shade he would have lost his shadow, nor that by resting quietly he would cease making footprints. He really was a great fool!

'You, Sir, try to distinguish the spheres of benevolence and righteousness, to explore the boundaries between agreement and disagreement, to study changes between rest and movement, to pontificate on giving and receiving, to order what is to be approved of and what disapproved of, to unify the limits of joy and anger, and yet you have barely escaped calamity. If you were to be serious in your cultivation of your own self, careful to guard the truth and willing to allow others to be as they are, then you could have avoided such problems. However, here you are, unable to cultivate yourself yet determined to improve others. Are you not obsessed with external things?'

Confucius, really cast down, said, 'Can I ask you about truth?'

'True truth is simple purity at its most perfect,' replied the stranger. 'To be without purity, to be without sincerity means you cannot move other people. So if you fake mourning and weeping, then no matter how thoroughly you do this, it's not real grief. If you make yourself act angry, even if you sound very fierce, this won't inspire awe. If you force yourself to be affectionate, no matter how much you smile, you cannot create harmony. True grief may make no sound but is really sorrowful; true anger, even if there is no manifestation of it, creates awe; true affection doesn't even need to smile but creates harmony. When someone has truth within, it affects his external spirit, which is why truth is so important.

PART 14
Epilogue

Chuang Tzu said, 'To know the Tao is easy, not to speak about it is hard. Knowing and not saying, this is to aspire to the Heavenly. Knowing and saying, this is to be subject to the human element. In the past people paid attention to the Heavenly, not to the human.'

[. . .]

A man from Sung, called Tsao Shang, was sent by the King of Sung as an ambassador to the state of Chin. When he left Sung he was given only a few carriages. However, the King of Chin was so delighted with him that he gave him a hundred more. On returning to Sung he met Chuang Tzu and said, 'Living in poor streets of an impoverished village, making sandals and starving, with a shrivelled neck and a sickly face, this I cannot stand! But being in the confidence of a ruler of ten thousand chariots and being given a hundred of them, this I enjoy and am good at.'

Chuang Tzu said, 'Well now. When the King of Chin falls ill, he summons his doctor who lances the ulcer or squeezes the boil and as a reward receives one carriage. The doctor who applies a suppository gets five carriages. The lower down the service, the more carriages given. So, Sir, I assume you must at least have been licking his piles to have been given so many carriages? Be gone, Sir!'

[. . .]

Someone offered Chuang Tzu a court post. Chuang Tzu answered the messenger, 'Sir, have you ever seen a sacrificial ox? It is decked in fine garments and fed on fresh grass and beans. However, when it is led into the Great Temple, even though it most earnestly might wish to be a simple calf again, it's now impossible!'

Chuang Tzu was dying and his followers wanted to provide a glorious funeral. Chuang Tzu said, 'I will have Heaven and Earth as my shroud and coffin; the sun and moon as my symbols of jade; the stars for my pearls and jewels; all the forms of life as my mourners. I have everything for my funeral, what is there missing? What more could I need?'

His followers said, 'We are worried, Master, that the crows and kites will eat you.'

'Above ground I shall be eaten by crows and kites,' said Chuang Tzu, 'and below ground by worms and ants. Aren't you just being rather partisan in wanting to feed only one of these groups, so depriving the others?

'Trying to use what isn't equal to produce equality is to be equally unequal. Trying to prove something by something uncertain is only certain to make things uncertain. The person whose eyesight is clear and thinks he understands is victim to these sights, whereas the one who is guided by the spirit perceives the reality. That there is a difference between what we see with our eyes and what we know through our spirit is a wisdom from long ago. But the fool relies upon his eyes and loses himself in what is merely human, and everything he does is just a façade – how sad!'

[. . .]

'The blank and the motionless have no form;
change and transformation are never at rest;
what is death?
what is life?
what is the companionship of Heaven and Earth?
where does the spirit of clarity go?
when forgotten, what becomes of it?

All forms of life are gathered around us, yet none of them is our destination. In the past people thought this was the way of the Tao. Chuang Tzu heard of these ideas and was pleased. He taught them using strange and mysterious expressions, wild and extraordinary phrases, and terms which had no precise meaning. He taught what he believed, yet was never partisan, nor did he view things from just one perspective. He saw the whole world as lost in foolishness and thus incapable of understanding anything sensible.

References

These extracts are taken from the Penguin Classics edition of *The Book of Chuang Tzu*. Part 1 is from chapter 2; part 2 from chapters 3, 4 and 5; part 3 from chapter 6; part 4 from chapters 7 and 8; part 5 from chapters 1, 5, 17, 18, 24 and 26; part 6 from chapter 9; part 7 from chapters 10 and 11; part 8 from chapters 11, 12 and 13; part 9 from chapters 14 and 16; part 10 from chapters 17 and 18; part 11 from chapters 19, 20 and 21; part 12 from chapters 22, 23, 24 and 26; part 13 from chapter 30 and 31; part 14 from chapters 32 and 33.

THE STORY OF PENGUIN CLASSICS

Before 1946 ... 'Classics' are mainly the domain of academics and students; readable editions for everyone else are almost unheard of. This all changes when a little-known classicist, E. V. Rieu, presents Penguin founder Allen Lane with the translation of Homer's *Odyssey* that he has been working on in his spare time.

1946 Penguin Classics debuts with *The Odyssey*, which promptly sells three million copies. Suddenly, classics are no longer for the privileged few.

1950s Rieu, now series editor, turns to professional writers for the best modern, readable translations, including Dorothy L. Sayers's *Inferno* and Robert Graves's unexpurgated *Twelve Caesars*.

1960s The Classics are given the distinctive black covers that have remained a constant throughout the life of the series. Rieu retires in 1964, hailing the Penguin Classics list as 'the greatest educative force of the twentieth century.'

1970s A new generation of translators swells the Penguin Classics ranks, introducing readers of English to classics of world literature from more than twenty languages. The list grows to encompass more history, philosophy, science, religion and politics.

1980s The Penguin American Library launches with titles such as *Uncle Tom's Cabin*, and joins forces with Penguin Classics to provide the most comprehensive library of world literature available from any paperback publisher.

1990s The launch of Penguin Audiobooks brings the classics to a listening audience for the first time, and in 1999 the worldwide launch of the Penguin Classics website extends their reach to the global online community.

The 21st Century Penguin Classics are completely redesigned for the first time in nearly twenty years. This world-famous series now consists of more than 1300 titles, making the widest range of the best books ever written available to millions – and constantly redefining what makes a 'classic'.

The Odyssey continues ...

The best books ever written

PENGUIN ⟨Ⓟ⟩ CLASSICS

SINCE 1946